The Essence of Jane Addams's
Twenty Years at Hull House

The Essence of
Jane Addams's
Twenty Years at Hull House

Edited with an Introduction by
Hunter Lewis

AXIOS

The Essence of . . . series of books are edited versions of great works of moral philosophy, distilled to reveal the essence of their authors' thought and argument. To read the complete, unedited version of this work, and see the excised passages, please visit our website at www.AxiosInstitute.org.

Axios Press
P.O. Box 118
Mount Jackson, VA 22842
888.542.9467   info@axiosinstitute.org

Library of Congress Cataloging-in-Publication Data

 Addams, Jane, 1860-1935.
 [Twenty years at Hull-House]
 The essence of Jane Addams's Twenty years at Hull House / edited, with an introduction, by Hunter Lewis.
 p. cm.—(The essence of—series)
 Originally published: New York : Signet Classics, 1961.
 Includes index.
 ISBN 978-1-60419-054-0 (pbk.)
 1. Hull House (Chicago, Ill.)—History. 2. Social settlements—Illinois—Chicago—History. 3. Addams, Jane, 1860–1935. 4.
 Women social reformers—United States—Biography. 5. Social service—Illinois—Chicago—History. I. Lewis, Hunter. II. Title.

 HV4196.C4A3 2012
 361.92–dc23
 [B]

             2011047059

Contents

Introduction

JANE ADDAMS (1860–1935) was arguably the most influential woman in American history. In 1897 she founded Hull House, a "settlement house" intended to serve the poor of Chicago, and lived there the rest of her life.

As time passed, she became a spokesperson for the poor, for women, for children, for families, for sanitation, for public health, for social and political reform, first in Chicago, then nationally, and finally throughout the world. In her time, she was as famous as a president, and her books were read everywhere.

Concern for the poor and minorities led her gradually into active politics. This included, in addition to municipal reform, winning voting rights for women and also a pacifist approach to world affairs. In 1931, she became the first American woman to win the Nobel Peace Prize.

Addams was among the first female American public intellectuals, and a hugely successful activist and reformer as well. Many in her own day and later regarded her, in addition, as a kind of secular saint. Her story shines forth brightly in her inspiring and easy-to-read autobiography.

In her early days, the future "saint" resisted efforts to mold her into a professing Christian, or alternatively, into a socialist. She complained of the "wilderness of dogma."* But she did eventually become a member of the Presbyterian Church. At first, on leaving college, she thought she would "study medicine and 'live with the poor.' "† She gave up the first ambition, but the second stayed with her during a few years of wandering around Europe with her lifelong friend, companion, and later deputy, Ellen Starr.

A particular incident deepened her resolve. In London she

> saw for the first time the overcrowded quarters of a great city at midnight. A small party of tourists were taken to the East End by a city missionary to witness the Saturday night sale of decaying vegetables and fruit, which, owing to the Sunday laws in London, could

---

* Hunter Lewis ed., *The Essence of Jane Addams's Twenty Years at Hull House*, (Mt. Jackson, VA: Axios Press, 2012), 43.

† Ibid, 46.

not be sold until Monday, and, as they were beyond safekeeping, were disposed of at auction as late as possible on Saturday night. On Mile End Road, from the top of an omnibus which paused at the end of a dingy street lighted by only occasional flares of gas, we saw two huge masses of ill-clad people clamoring around two hucksters' carts. They were bidding their farthings and ha'pennies for a vegetable held up by the auctioneer, which he at last scornfully flung, with a gibe for its cheapness, to the successful bidder. In the momentary pause only one man detached himself from the groups. He had bidden in a cabbage, and when it struck his hand, he instantly sat down on the curb, tore it with his teeth, and hastily devoured it, unwashed and uncooked as it was. . . . The final impression was not of ragged, tawdry clothing nor of pinched and sallow faces, but of myriads of hands, empty, pathetic, nerveless, and work worn, showing white in the uncertain light of the street, and clutching forward for food which was already unfit to eat. . . .

During her years of finding herself, Addams was often plagued by a variety of illnesses, some related to a congenital back deformity, and by nervous exhaustion. Money she did not lack, because she was the sole heir of a successful, self-made, rural Illinois merchant. But even the question of how to spend and how to invest her fortune posed problems:

> In one of the . . . summers between . . . European journeys I visited a western state where I had formerly invested a sum of money in mortgages. I was much horrified by the wretched conditions among the farmers, which had resulted from a long period of drought, and one forlorn picture was fairly burned into my mind. A number of starved hogs—collateral for a promissory note—were huddled into an open pen. Their backs were humped in a curious, camel-like fashion, and they were devouring one of their own number, the latest victim of absolute starvation or possibly merely the one least able to defend himself against their voracious hunger. The farmer's wife looked on indifferently, a picture of despair as she stood in the door of the bare, crude house, and the two children behind her, whom she vainly tried to keep out of sight, continually thrust forward their faces almost covered by masses of coarse, sunburned hair, and their little bare feet

so black, so hard, the great cracks so filled with dust that they looked like flattened hoofs. The children could not be compared to anything so joyous as satyrs, although they appeared but half-human. It seemed to me quite impossible to receive interest from mortgages placed upon farms which might at any season be reduced to such conditions, and with great inconvenience to my agent and doubtless with hardship to the farmers, as speedily as possible I withdrew all my investment.

In founding Hull House, Addams discovered that her own funds did not go very far. As she coolly notes:

We were often bitterly pressed for money and worried by the prospect of unpaid bills, and we gave up one golden scheme after another because we could not afford it; we cooked the meals and kept the books and washed the windows without a thought of hardship if we thereby saved money for the consummation of some ardently desired undertaking.

Hull House was modeled after Toynbee Hall in London. Each day it opened its doors to mothers leaving children in a nursery, to young and old people coming to classes and social clubs, and to people seeking assistance. As Addams describes it:

The memory of the first years at Hull House is more or less blurred with fatigue, for we could of course become accustomed only gradually to the unending activity and to the confusion of a house constantly filling and refilling with groups of people.

There were many gratifying successes. Boys kept off the streets were not arrested for juvenile offenses. Girls were protected from prostitution rings. An uncaring and unresponsive city bureaucracy was forced to respond a little more. Deserted wives and bewildered widows were given some assistance. Recalcitrant pharmacists were stopped from selling cocaine to minors; garment sweat shops were stopped from sending out smallpox infected garments. One of the greatest triumphs was the long drawn out battle to clean up the fetid streets piled high with garbage and human sewage, all of which contributed to a high death toll. As Addams writes:

Possibly our efforts slightly modified the worst conditions, but they still remained intolerable, and the fourth summer the situation became for me absolutely desperate when I realized in a moment of panic that my delicate little nephew for whom I was guardian, could not be with me at Hull House at all unless the sickening odors were reduced. I may well be ashamed that other delicate children who were torn from their families, not into boarding school but into eternity, had not long before driven me to effective action. Under the direction of the first man who came as a resident to Hull House, we began a systematic investigation of the city system of garbage collection, both as to its efficiency in other wards and its possible connection with the death rate in the various wards of the city.

The Hull House Woman's Club had been organized the year before by the resident kindergartner who had first inaugurated a mother's meeting. The new members came together, however, in quite a new way that summer when we discussed with them the high death rate so persistent in our ward. After several club meetings devoted to the subject, despite the fact that the death rate rose highest in the congested foreign colonies and not in the streets in which most of the Irish American club women lived, twelve of their number undertook, in connection with the residents, to carefully investigate the conditions of the alleys. During August and September, the substantiated reports of violations of the law sent in from Hull House to the health department were one thousand and thirty-seven. For the club woman who had finished a long day's work of washing or ironing followed by the cooking of a hot supper, it would have been much easier to sit on her doorstep during a summer evening than to go up and down ill-kept alleys and get into trouble with her neighbors over the condition of their garbage boxes. It required both civic enterprise and moral conviction to be willing to do this three evenings a week during the hottest and most uncomfortable months of the year. Nevertheless, a certain number of women persisted, as did the residents, and three city inspectors in succession were transferred from the ward because of unsatisfactory services. Still the death rate remained high and the condition seemed little improved throughout the next winter. In sheer desperation, the following spring when the city contracts were awarded for the removal of garbage, with the backing of two well-known businessmen, I put in a bid for the garbage removal of the nineteenth ward. My paper was thrown out on a technicality but the incident induced the mayor to appoint me the garbage inspector of the ward.

The salary was a thousand dollars a year, and the loss of that political "plum" made a great stir among the politicians. The position was no sinecure whether regarded from the point of view of getting up at six in the morning to see that the men were early at work; or of following the loaded wagons, uneasily dropping their contents at intervals, to their dreary destination at the dump; or of insisting that the contractor must increase the number of his wagons from nine to thirteen and from thirteen to seventeen, although he assured me that he lost money on every one and that the former inspector had let him off with seven; or of taking careless landlords into court because they would not provide the proper garbage receptacles; or of arresting the tenant who tried to make the garbage wagons carry away the contents of his stable.

With the two or three residents who nobly stood by, we set up six of those doleful incinerators which are supposed to burn garbage with the fuel collected in the alley itself. The one factory in town which could utilize old tin cans was a window weight factory, and we deluged that with ten times as many tin cans as it could use—much less would pay for. We made desperate attempts to have the dead animals removed by the contractor who was paid most liberally by the city for that purpose but who, we slowly discovered, always made the police ambulances do the work, delivering the carcasses upon freight cars for shipment to a soap factory in Indiana where they were sold for a good price although the contractor himself was the largest stockholder in the concern.

Careful inspection combined with other causes, brought about a great improvement in the cleanliness and comfort of the neighborhood and one happy day, when the death rate of our ward was found to have dropped from third to seventh in the list of city wards and was so reported to our Woman's Club, the applause which followed recorded the genuine sense of participation in the result, and a public spirit which had "made good."

But the cleanliness of the ward was becoming much too popular to suit our all-powerful alderman and, although we felt fatuously secure under the regime of civil service, he found a way to circumvent us by eliminating the position altogether. He introduced an ordinance into the city council which combined the collection of refuse with the cleaning and repairing of the streets, the whole to be placed under a ward superintendent. The office of course was to be filled under civil service regulations but only men were eligible to the examination. Although this latter regulation was afterwards modified in favor of one woman, it was retained long enough to put the nineteenth ward inspector out of office. . . .

In the summer of 1902 during an epidemic of typhoid fever in which our ward, although containing but one thirty-sixth of the population of the city, registered one sixth of the total number of deaths, two of the Hull House residents made an investigation of the methods of plumbing in the houses adjacent to conspicuous groups of fever cases.

The agitation finally resulted in a long and stirring trial before the civil service board of half of the employees in the Sanitary Bureau, with the final discharge of eleven out of the entire force of twenty-four. The inspector in our neighborhood was a kindly old man, greatly distressed over the affair, and quite unable to understand why he should have not used his discretion as to the time when a landlord should be forced to put in modern appliances. If he was "very poor," or "just about to sell his place," or "sure that the house would be torn down to make room for a factory," why should one "inconvenience" him? The old man died soon after the trial, feeling persecuted to the very last and not in the least understanding what it was all about. We were amazed at the commercial ramifications which graft in the city hall involved and at the indignation which interference with it produced. Hull House lost some large subscriptions as the result of this investigation, a loss which, if not easy to bear, was at least comprehensible. We also uncovered unexpected graft in connection with the plumbers' unions, and but for the fearless testimony of one of their members, could never have brought the trial to a successful issue.

There were many instances where Addams could do nothing, try as she might. There is the pathetic story of the mother wetting herself at work while her baby starved:

I was detained late one evening in an office building by a prolonged committee meeting of the Board of Education. As I came out at eleven o'clock, I met in the corridor of the fourteenth floor a woman whom I knew, on her knees scrubbing the marble tiling. As she straightened up to greet me, she seemed so wet from her feet up to her chin, that I hastily inquired the cause. Her reply was that she left home at five o'clock every night and had no opportunity for six hours to nurse her baby. Her mother's milk mingled with the very water with which she scrubbed the floors until she should return at midnight, heated and exhausted, to feed her screaming child with what remained within her breasts. . . .

Equally heart rending is the story of "Goosie" and his mother:

I recall . . . the mother of "Goosie," as the children for years called a little boy who, because he was brought to the nursery wrapped up in his mother's shawl, always had his hair filled with the down and small feathers from the feather brush factory where she worked. One March morning, Goosie's mother was hanging out the washing on a shed roof before she left for the factory. Five-year-old Goosie was trotting at her heels handing her clothes pins, when he was suddenly blown off the roof by the high wind into the alley below. His neck was broken by the fall, and as he lay piteous and limp on a pile of frozen refuse, his mother cheerily called him to "climb up again," so confident do overworked mothers become that their children cannot get hurt. After the funeral, as the poor mother sat in the nursery postponing the moment when she must go back to her empty rooms, I asked her, in a futile effort to be of comfort, if there was anything more we could do for her. The overworked, sorrow-stricken woman looked up and replied, "If you could give me my wages for tomorrow, I would not go to work in the factory at all. I would like to stay at home all day and hold the baby. Goosie was always asking me to take him and I never had any time." This statement revealed the condition of many nursery mothers who are obliged to forego the joys and solaces which belong to even the most poverty-stricken. The long hours of factory labor necessary for earning the support of a child leave no time for the tender care and caressing which may enrich the life of the most piteous baby.

If small children were not left alone in tenements for most of the day, they were often made to work themselves:

> The visits we made in the neighborhood constantly discovered women sewing upon sweatshop work, and often they were assisted by incredibly small children. I remember a little girl of four who pulled out basting threads hour after hour, sitting on a stool at the feet of her Bohemian mother, a little bunch of human misery. But even for that there was no legal redress, for the only child-labor law in Illinois, with any provision for enforcement, had been secured by the coal miners' unions, and was confined to children employed in mines.

> There was at that time no statistical information on Chicago industrial conditions, and Mrs. Florence Kelley, an early resident of Hull House, suggested to the Illinois State Bureau of Labor that they investigate the sweating system in Chicago with its attendant child labor. The head of the Bureau adopted this suggestion and engaged Mrs. Kelley to make the investigation. When the report was presented to the Illinois Legislature, a special committee was appointed to

look into the Chicago conditions. I well recall that on the Sunday the members of this commission came to dine at Hull House, our hopes ran high, and we believed that at last some of the worst ills under which our neighbors were suffering would be brought to an end.

As a result of its investigations, this committee recommended to the Legislature the provisions which afterward became those of the first factory law of Illinois, regulating the sanitary conditions of the sweatshop and fixing fourteen as the age at which a child might be employed.

It was, perhaps, a premature effort, though certainly founded upon a genuine need, to urge that a clause limiting the hours of all women working in factories or workshops to eight a day, or forty-eight a week, should be inserted in the first factory legislation of the State. . . .

The eight-hour clause . . . met with much less opposition in the Legislature than was anticipated, and was enforced for a year before it was pronounced unconstitutional by the Supreme Court of Illinois. . . .

So Jane Addams's life went. Two steps forward, one back, all in a ceaseless swirl of activity. She was admired, even lionized. She was also reviled, condemned as a radical or even an anarchist. Later in life, her embrace of the worldwide pacifist movement after World War I, embroiled her in further controversy. But, throughout it all, her reputation, her standing, her fame, just kept spreading, along with her combination of Christian charity with political reform, until she became one of the most celebrated, and one of the most justly celebrated, figures of American history.

—Hunter Lewis

To the Memory of My Father

Preface

MANY TIMES DURING the writing of these reminiscences, I have become convinced that the task was undertaken all too soon. One's fiftieth year is indeed an impressive milestone at which one may well pause to take an accounting. . . .

It has. . . been hard to determine what incidents and experiences should be selected for recital, and . . . for . . . this reason . . . and many others I have found it difficult to make a faithful record of the years since the autumn of 1889 when without any preconceived social theories or economic views, I came to live in an industrial district of Chicago. . . .

Chapter One

Earliest Impressions

I BEGIN THIS RECORD with some impressions of my childhood. . . . All of these are directly connected with my father. . . .

It must have been from a very early period that I recall "horrid nights" when I tossed about in my bed because I had told a lie. I was held in the grip of a miserable dread of death, a double fear, first, that I myself should die in my sins and go straight to that fiery Hell which was never mentioned at home, but which I had heard all about from other children, and, second, that my father—representing the entire adult world which I had basely deceived—should himself die before I had time to tell him. My only method of obtaining relief was to go downstairs to my father's room and make full confession. The high resolve to do this would push me out of bed and carry me down the stairs. . . . I would finally reach my father's bedside perfectly breathless and having panted out the history of my sin, invariably received the same assurance that if he "had a little girl who told lies," he was very glad that she "felt too bad to go to sleep afterward." . . .

My great veneration and pride in my father manifested itself in curious ways. On several Sundays, doubtless occurring in two or three different years, the Union Sunday School of the village was visited by strangers. . . . My father taught the large Bible class in the left-hand corner of the church next to the pulpit, and to my eyes at least, was a most imposing figure in his Sunday frock coat, his fine head rising high above all the others. I imagined that the strangers were filled with admiration for this dignified person, and I prayed with all my heart that the ugly, pigeon-toed little girl, whose crooked back obliged her to walk with her head held very much upon one side, would never be pointed out to these visitors as the daughter of this fine man. . . .

. . . The house at the end of the village in which I was born, and which was my home until I moved to Hull House, in my earliest childhood had opposite to it—only across the road and then across a little stretch of greensward—two mills belonging to my father; one flour mill, to which the various grains were brought by the neighboring farmers, and one sawmill, in which the logs of the native timber were sawed into lumber. The latter offered the great excitement of sitting on a log while it slowly approached the buzzing saw which was cutting it into slabs, and of getting off just in time to escape a sudden and gory death. But the flouring mill was much more beloved. It was full of dusky, floury places which we adored, of empty bins in which we might play house; it had a basement, with piles of bran and shorts which were almost as good as sand to play in. . . .

In addition to these fascinations was the association of the mill with my father's activities, for doubtless at that time I centered upon him all that careful imitation which a little girl ordinarily gives to her mother's ways and habits. My mother had died when I was a baby and my father's second marriage did not occur until my eighth year. . . .

. . . In this case, too, I doubtless contributed my share to that stream of admiration which our generation so generously poured forth for the self-made man. I was consumed by a wistful desire to apprehend the hardships of my father's earlier life in that faraway time when he had been a miller's apprentice. I knew that he still woke up punctually at three o'clock because for so many years he had taken his turn at the mill in the early morning, and if by chance I awoke at the same hour, as curiously enough I often did, I imagined him in the early dawn in my uncle's old mill reading through the entire village library, book after book, beginning with the lives of the signers of the Declaration of Independence. . . .

Although I constantly confided my sins and perplexities to my father, there are only a few occasions on which I remember having received direct advice or admonition. . . . I can remember an admonition on one occasion, however, when, as a little girl of eight years, arrayed in a new cloak, gorgeous beyond anything I had ever worn before, I stood before my father for his approval. I was much chagrined by his remark that it was a very pretty cloak—in fact so much prettier than any cloak the other little girls in the Sunday School had, that he would advise me to wear my old cloak, which would keep me quite as warm, with the added advantage of not making the other little girls feel bad. . . . As I walked soberly through the village street by the side of my counselor, my mind was busy . . . with the old question eternally suggested by the inequalities of the human lot. Only as we neared the church door did I venture to ask what could be done about it, receiving the reply that it might never be righted so far as clothes went, but that people might be equal in things that mattered much more than clothes, the affairs of education and religion, for instance. . . .

I recall with great distinctness my first direct contact with death when I was fifteen years old: Polly was an old nurse who had taken care of my mother and had followed her to frontier Illinois to help rear a second generation of children. She had always lived in our house, but made annual visits to her cousins on a farm a few miles north of the village. During one of those visits, word came to us one Sunday evening that Polly was dying, and for a number of reasons I was the only person able to go to her. I left the lamp-lit, warm house to be driven four miles through a blinding storm which every minute added more snow to the already high drifts, with a sense of starting upon a fateful errand. An hour after my arrival all of the cousin's family went downstairs to supper, and I was left alone to watch with Polly. The square, old-fashioned chamber in the lonely farmhouse was very cold and still, with nothing to be heard but the storm outside. Suddenly the great change came. I heard a feeble call of "Sarah," my mother's name, as the dying eyes were turned upon me, followed by a curious breathing and in place of the face familiar from my earliest childhood and associated with homely household cares, there lay upon the pillow strange, august features, stern and withdrawn from all the small affairs of life. . . .

Perhaps I may record here my protest against the efforts, so often made, to shield children and young people from all that has to do with death and sorrow, to give them a good time at all hazards on the assumption that the ills of life will come soon enough. Young people themselves often resent this attitude on the part of their elders; they feel set aside and belittled as if they were denied the common human experiences. They too wish to climb steep stairs and to eat their bread with tears. . . .

Chapter Two

Influence of Lincoln

I WAS BUT FOUR and a half years old when Lincoln died. I distinctly remember the day when I found on our two white gateposts American flags companioned with black. I tumbled down on the harsh gravel walk in my eager rush into the house to inquire what they were "there for." To my amazement I found my father in tears, something that I had never seen before, having assumed, as all children do, that grown-up people never cried. The two flags, my father's tears, and his impressive statement that the greatest man in the world had died, constituted my initiation, my baptism, as it were, into the thrilling and solemn interests of a world lying quite outside the two white gateposts. . . . A gentle old lady . . . lived in a white farmhouse a mile north of the village.

She was the mother of the village hero, Tommy, and used to tell us of her long anxiety during the spring of 1862; how she waited day after day for the hospital to surrender up her son, each morning airing the white homespun sheets and holding the little bedroom in immaculate readiness. It was after the battle of Fort Donelson that Tommy was wounded and had been taken to the hospital at Springfield; his father went down to him and saw him getting worse each week, until it was clear that he was going to die; but there was so much red tape about the department, and affairs were so confused, that his discharge could not be procured. At last the hospital surgeon intimated to his father that he should quietly take him away; a man as sick as that, it would be all right; but when they told Tommy, weak as he was, his eyes flashed, and he said, "No, sir; I will go out of the front door or I'll die here." Of course after that every man in the hospital worked for it, and in two weeks he was honorably discharged. When he came home at last, his mother's heart was broken to see him so wan and changed. She would tell us of the long quiet days that followed his return, with the windows open so that the dying eyes might look over the orchard slope to the meadow beyond where the younger brothers were mowing the early hay. She told us of those days when his school friends from the Academy flocked in to see him, their old acknowledged leader, and of the burning words of earnest patriotism spoken in the crowded little room, so that in three months the Academy was almost deserted and the new Company who marched away in the autumn took as drummer boy Tommy's third brother, who was only seventeen and too young for a regular. She remembered the still darker days that followed, when the bright drummer boy was in Andersonville prison, and little by little she learned to be reconciled that Tommy was safe in the peaceful home graveyard.

However much we were given to talk of war heroes, we always fell silent as we approached an isolated farmhouse in which two old people lived alone. Five of their sons had enlisted in the Civil War, and only the youngest had returned alive in the spring of 1865. In the autumn of the same year, when he was hunting for wild ducks in a swamp on the rough little farm itself, he was accidentally shot and killed, and the old people were left alone to struggle with the half-cleared land as best they might. When we were driven past this forlorn little farm our childish voices always dropped into speculative whisperings as to how the accident could have happened to this remaining son out of all the men in the world, to him who had escaped so many chances of death! Our young hearts swelled in first rebellion against that which Walter Pater calls "the inexplicable shortcoming or misadventure on the part of life itself";

we were overwhelmingly oppressed by that grief of things as they are, so much more mysterious and intolerable than those griefs which we think dimly to trace to man's own wrongdoing.

It was well perhaps that life thus early gave me a hint of one of her most obstinate and insoluble riddles, for I have sorely needed the sense of universality thus imparted to that mysterious injustice, the burden of which we are all forced to bear and with which I have become only too familiar. . . .

Thousands of children in the sixties and seventies, in the simplicity which is given to the understanding of a child, caught a notion of imperishable heroism when they were told that brave men had lost their lives that the slaves might be free. At any moment the conversation of our elders might turn upon these heroic events; there were red-letter days, when a certain general came to see my father, and again when Governor Oglesby, whom all Illinois children called "Uncle Dick," spent a Sunday under the pine trees in our front yard. We felt on those days a connection with the great world so much more heroic than the village world which surrounded us through all the other days. My father was a member of the state senate for the sixteen years between 1854 and 1870, and even as a little child I was dimly conscious of the grave march of public affairs in his comings and goings at the state capital.

He was much too occupied to allow time for reminiscence, but I remember overhearing a conversation between a visitor and himself concerning the stirring days before the war, when it was by no means certain that the Union men in the legislature would always have enough votes to keep Illinois from seceding. I heard with breathless interest my father's account of the trip a majority of the legislators had made one dark day to St. Louis, that there might not be enough men for a quorum, and so no vote could be taken on the momentous question until the Union men could rally their forces.

My father always spoke of the martyred President as Mr. Lincoln, and I never heard the great name without a thrill. I remember the day—it must have been one of comparative leisure, perhaps a Sunday—when at my request my father took out of his desk a thin packet marked "Mr. Lincoln's Letters," the shortest one of which bore unmistakable traces of that remarkable personality. These letters began, "My dear Double-D'ed Addams," and to the inquiry as to how the person thus addressed was about to vote on a certain measure then before the legislature, was added the assurance that he knew that this Addams "would vote according to his conscience," but he begged to know in which direction the same conscience "was pointing." As my father folded up the bits of paper I fairly held my breath in my desire that he should go on with the reminiscence of this wonderful man, whom he had known in his comparative obscurity, or better still, that he should be moved to tell some of the exciting incidents of the Lincoln-Douglas debates. There were at least two pictures of Lincoln that always hung in my father's room, and one in our old-fashioned upstairs parlor, of Lincoln with little Tad. . . .

Of the many things written of my father in that sad August in 1881, when he died, the one I cared for most was written by an old political friend of his who was then editor of a great Chicago daily. He wrote that while there were doubtless many members of the Illinois legislature who during the great contracts of the war time and the demoralizing reconstruction days that followed, had never accepted a bribe, he wished to bear testimony that he personally had known but this one man who had never been offered a bribe because bad men were instinctively afraid of him.

I feel now the hot chagrin with which I recalled this statement during those early efforts of Illinois in which Hull House joined, to secure the passage of the first factory legislation. I was told by the representatives of an informal association of manufacturers that if the residents of Hull House would drop this nonsense about a sweatshop bill, of which they knew nothing, certain businessmen would agree to give fifty thousand dollars within two years to be used for any of the philanthropic activities of the Settlement.

As the fact broke upon me that I was being offered a bribe, the shame was enormously increased by the memory of this statement. What had befallen the daughter of my father that such a thing could happen to her? The salutary reflection that it could not have occurred unless a weakness in myself had permitted it, withheld me at least from an historic display of indignation before the two men making the offer, and I explained as gently as I could that we had no ambition to make Hull House "the largest institution on the West Side," but that we were much concerned that our neighbors should be protected from untoward conditions of work, and—so much heroics, youth must permit itself—if to accomplish this the destruction of Hull House was necessary, that we would cheerfully sing a Te Deum on its ruins. . . .

Chapter Three

Boarding School Ideals

THE SCHOOL AT Rockford in 1877 had not changed its name from seminary to college, although it numbered, on its faculty and among its alumnae, college women who were most eager that this should be done, and who really accomplished it during the next five years. The school was one of the earliest efforts for women's higher education in the Mississippi Valley, and from the beginning was called "The Mount Holyoke of the West." It reflected much of the missionary spirit of that pioneer institution, and the proportion of missionaries among its early graduates was almost as large as Mount Holyoke's own. In addition there had been thrown about the founders of the early western school the glamour of frontier privations, and the first students, conscious of the heroic self-sacrifice made in their behalf, felt that each minute of the time thus dearly bought must be conscientiously used. . . .

There were practically no Economics taught in women's colleges—at least in the freshwater ones— thirty years ago, although we painstakingly studied "Mental" and "Moral" Philosophy, which, though far from dry in the classroom, became the subject of more spirited discussion outside, and gave us a clue for animated rummaging in the little college library. Of course we read a great deal of Ruskin and Browning, and liked the most abstruse parts the best; but like the famous gentleman who talked prose without knowing it, we never dreamed of connecting them with our philosophy. My genuine interest was history, partly because of a superior teacher, and partly because my father had always insisted upon a certain amount of historic reading ever since he had paid me, as a little girl, five cents a "Life" for each Plutarch hero I could intelligently report to him and twenty-five cents for every volume of Irving's *Life of Washington*.

When we started for the long vacations, a little group of five would vow that during the summer we would read all of Motley's *Dutch Republic* or, more ambitious still, all of Gibbon's *Decline and Fall of the Roman Empire*. When we returned at the opening of school and three of us announced we had finished the latter, each became skeptical of the other two. We fell

upon each other in a sort of rough-and-tumble examination, in which no quarter was given or received;
but the suspicion was finally removed that anyone
had skipped. . . .

Of course in such an atmosphere a girl like myself,
of serious not to say priggish tendency, did not escape
a concerted pressure to push her into the "missionary field." During the four years it was inevitable that
every sort of evangelical appeal should have been
made to reach the comparatively few "unconverted"
girls in the school. We were the subject of prayer at
the daily chapel exercise and the weekly prayer meeting, attendance upon which was obligatory.

I was singularly unresponsive to all these forms of
emotional appeal, although I became unspeakably
embarrassed when they were presented to me at close
range by a teacher during the "silent hour," which we
were all required to observe every evening, and which
was never broken into, even by a member of the faculty, unless the errand was one of grave import. I
found these occasional interviews on the part of one
of the more serious young teachers, of whom I was
extremely fond, hard to endure, as was a long series
of conversations in my senior year conducted by one
of the most enthusiastic members of the faculty, in
which the desirability of Turkey as a field for missionary labor was enticingly put before me. I suppose I
held myself aloof from all these influences, partly

owing to the fact that my father was not a communicant of any church, and I tremendously admired his scrupulous morality and sense of honor in all matters of personal and public conduct, and also because the little group to which I have referred was much given to a sort of rationalism, doubtless founded upon an early reading of Emerson. . . .

. . . The regime of Rockford Seminary was still very simple in the 1870s. Each student made her own fire and kept her own room in order. Sunday morning was a great clearing up day, and the sense of having made immaculate my own immediate surroundings, the consciousness of clean linen, said to be close to the consciousness of a clean conscience, always . . . remains in my mind. . . .

Throughout our school years, we were always keenly conscious of the growing development of Rockford Seminary into a college. The opportunity for our Alma Mater to take her place in the new movement of full college education for women filled us with enthusiasm, and it became a driving ambition with the undergraduates to share in this new and glorious undertaking. We gravely decided that it was important that some of the students should be ready to receive the bachelor's degree the very first moment that the charter of the school should secure the right to confer it. Two of us, therefore, took a course in mathematics, advanced beyond anything previously given in the school, from one of those early young women working for a PhD, who was temporarily teaching in Rockford that she might study more mathematics in Leipzig. . . .

In line with this policy of placing a woman's college on an equality with the other colleges of the state, we applied for an opportunity to compete in the intercollegiate oratorical contest of Illinois, and we succeeded in having Rockford admitted as the first woman's college. When I was finally selected as the orator, I was somewhat dismayed to find that, representing not only one school but college women in general, I could not resent the brutal frankness with which my oratorical possibilities were discussed by the enthusiastic group who would allow no personal feeling to stand in the way of progress, especially the progress of Woman's Cause. I was told among other things that I had an intolerable habit of dropping my voice at the end of a sentence in the most feminine, apologetic and even deprecatory manner which would probably lose Woman the first place.

Woman certainly did lose the first place and stood fifth, exactly in the dreary middle. . . .

. . . Our aspiring college . . . did not fail to make me realize that I had dealt the cause of woman's advancement a staggering blow, and all my explanations of the fifth place were haughtily considered insufficient before that golden Bar of Youth, so absurdly inflexible!

To return to my last year of school, it was inevitable that the pressure toward religious profession should increase as graduating day approached. So curious, however, are the paths of moral development that several times during subsequent experiences have I felt that this passive resistance of mine, this clinging to an individual conviction, was the best moral training I received at Rockford College. During the first decade of Hull House, it was felt by propagandists of diverse social theories that the new Settlement would be a fine coign of vantage from which to propagate social faiths, and that a mere preliminary step would be the conversion of the founders; hence I have been reasoned with hours at a time, and I recall at least three occasions when this was followed by actual prayer. In the first instance, the honest exhorter who fell upon his knees before my astonished eyes was an advocate of single tax upon land values. He begged, in that phraseology which is deemed appropriate for prayer, that "the sister might see the beneficent results it would bring to the poor who live in the awful congested districts around this very house."

The early socialists used every method of attack—a favorite one being the statement, doubtless sometimes honestly made, that I really was a socialist, but "too much of a coward to say so." I remember one socialist who habitually opened a very telling address he was in the habit of giving upon the street corners, by holding me up as an awful example to his fellow socialists, as one of their number "who had been caught in the toils of capitalism." He always added as a final clinching of the statement that he knew what he was talking about because he was a member of the Hull House Men's Club. When I ventured to say to him that not all of the thousands of people who belong to a class or club at Hull House could possibly know my personal opinions, and to mildly inquire upon what he founded his assertions, he triumphantly replied that I had once admitted to him that I had read Sombart and Loria, and that anyone of sound mind must see the inevitable conclusions of such master reasonings.

I could multiply these two instances a hundredfold, and possibly nothing aided me to stand on my own feet and to select what seemed reasonable from this wilderness of dogma, so much as my early encounter with genuine zeal and affectionate solicitude, associated with what I could not accept as the whole truth.

I do not wish to take callow writing too seriously, but I reproduce from an oratorical contest the following bit of premature pragmatism. . . . "Those who believe that Justice is but a poetical longing within us, the enthusiast who thinks it will come in the form of a millennium, those who see it established by the strong arm of a hero, are not those who have comprehended the vast truths of life. The actual Justice must come by trained intelligence, by broadened sympathies toward the individual man or woman who crosses our path; one item added to another is the only method by which to build up a conception lofty enough to be of use in the world."

This schoolgirl recipe has been tested in many later experiences, the most dramatic of which came when I was called upon by a manufacturing company to act as one of three arbitrators in a perplexing struggle between themselves, a group of trade unionists, and a nonunion employee of their establishment. The nonunion man who was the cause of the difficulty had ten years before sided with his employers in a prolonged strike and had bitterly fought the union. He had been so badly injured at that time, that in spite of long months of hospital care he had never afterward been able to do a full day's work, although his employers had retained him for a decade at full pay in recognition of his loyalty. At the end of ten years the once defeated union was strong enough to enforce its demands for a union shop and in spite of the distaste of the firm for the arrangement, no obstacle to harmonious relations with the union remained but for the refusal of the trade unionists to receive as one of their members the old crippled employee, whose spirit was broken at last and who was now willing to join the union and to stand with his old enemies for the sake of retaining his place.

But the union men would not receive "a traitor," the firm flatly refused to dismiss so faithful an employee, the busy season was upon them, and everyone concerned had finally agreed to abide without appeal by the decision of the arbitrators. The chairman of our little arbitration committee, a venerable judge, quickly demonstrated that it was impossible to collect trustworthy evidence in regards to the events already ten years old which lay at the bottom of this bitterness, and we soon therefore ceased to interview the conflicting witnesses; the second member of the committee sternly bade the men remember that the most ancient Hebraic authority gave no sanction for holding even a just resentment for more than seven years, and at last we all settled down to that wearisome effort to secure the inner consent of all concerned, upon which alone the "mystery of justice" as Maeterlinck has told us, ultimately depends. I am not quite sure that in the end we administered justice, but certainly employers, trade unionists, and arbitrators were all convinced that justice will have to be established in industrial affairs with the same care and patience which has been necessary for centuries in order to institute it in men's civic relationships, although as the judge remarked the search must be conducted without much help from precedent. The conviction remained with me, that however long a time might be required to establish justice in the new relationships of our raw industrialism, it would never be stable until it had received the sanction of those upon whom the present situation presses so harshly.

Towards the end of our four years' course we debated much as to what we were to be, and long before the end of my school days it was quite settled in my mind that I should study medicine and "live with the poor." This conclusion of course was the result of many things, perhaps epitomized in my graduating essay. . . .

. . . The essay contains . . . the statement that women can only "grow accurate and intelligible by the thorough study of at least one branch of physical science, for only with eyes thus accustomed to the search for truth can she detect all self-deceit and fancy in herself and learn to express herself without dogmatism." So much for the first part of the thesis. Having thus "gained accuracy, would woman bring this force to bear throughout morals and justice, then she must find in active labor the promptings and inspirations that come from growing insight. . . ."

This veneration for science portrayed in my final essay was doubtless the result of the statements the textbooks were then making of what was called the theory of evolution, the acceptance of which even thirty years after the publication of Darwin's *The Origin of Species* had about it a touch of intellectual adventure. . . . We chafed at the meagerness of the college library in this direction, and I used to bring back in my handbag books belonging to an advanced brother-in-law who had studied medicine in Germany and who therefore was quite emancipated. The first gift I made when I came into possession of my small estate the year after I left school, was a thousand dollars to the library of Rockford College, with the stipulation that it be spent for scientific books. . . .

We believed, in our sublime self-conceit, that the difficulty of life would lie solely in the direction of losing these precious ideals of ours, of failing to follow the way of martyrdom and high purpose we had marked out for ourselves. . . .

The year after I had left college I came back, with a classmate, to receive the degree we had so eagerly anticipated. Two of the graduating class were also ready and four of us were dubbed BA on the very day that Rockford Seminary was declared a college in the midst of tumultuous anticipations. Having had a year outside of college walls in that trying land between vague hope and definite attainment, I had become very much sobered in my desire for a degree, and was already beginning to emerge from that rose-colored mist with which the dream of youth so readily envelops the future.

. . . It required eight years—from the time I left Rockford in the summer of 1881 until Hull House was opened in the autumn of 1889—to formulate my convictions even in the least satisfactory manner, much less to reduce them to a plan for action. During most of that time I was absolutely at sea so far as any moral purpose was concerned, clinging only to the desire to live in a really living world and refusing to be content with a shadowy intellectual or aesthetic reflection of it.

Chapter Four

The Snare of Preparation

THE WINTER AFTER I left school was spent in the Woman's Medical College of Philadelphia, but the development of the spinal difficulty which had shadowed me from childhood forced me into Dr. Weir Mitchell's hospital for the late spring, and the next winter I was literally bound to a bed in my sister's house for six months. In spite of its tedium, the long winter had its mitigations, for after the first few weeks I was able to read with a luxurious consciousness of leisure, and I remember opening the first volume of Carlyle's *Frederick the Great* with a lively sense of gratitude that it was not *Gray's Anatomy*, having found, like many another, that general culture is a much easier undertaking than professional study. The long illness inevitably put aside the immediate prosecution of a medical course, and although I had passed my examinations creditably enough in the required subjects for the first year, I was very glad to have a physician's sanction for giving up clinics and dissecting rooms and to follow his prescription of spending the next two years in Europe.

Before I returned to America I had discovered that there were other genuine reasons for living among the poor than that of practicing medicine upon them, and my brief foray into the profession was never resumed.

The long illness left me in a state of nervous exhaustion with which I struggled for years, traces of it remaining long after Hull House was opened in 1889. At the best it allowed me but a limited amount of energy, so that doubtless there was much nervous depression at the foundation of the spiritual struggles which this chapter is forced to record. However, it could not have been all due to my health, for as my wise little notebook sententiously remarked, "In his own way each man must struggle, lest the moral law become a far-off abstraction utterly separated from his active life."

It would, of course, be impossible to remember that some of these struggles ever took place at all, were it not for these selfsame notebooks, in which, however, I no longer wrote in moments of high resolve, but judging from the internal evidence afforded by the books themselves, only in moments of deep depression when overwhelmed by a sense of failure.

One of the most poignant of these experiences, which occurred during the first few months after our landing upon the other side of the Atlantic, was on a Saturday night, when I received an ineradicable impression of the wretchedness of East London, and also saw for the first time the overcrowded quarters of a great city at midnight. A small party of tourists were taken to the East End by a city missionary to witness the Saturday night sale of decaying vegetables and fruit, which, owing to the Sunday laws in London, could not be sold until Monday, and, as they were beyond safekeeping, were disposed of at auction as late as possible on Saturday night. On Mile End Road, from the top of an omnibus which paused at the end of a dingy street lighted by only occasional flares of gas, we saw two huge masses of ill-clad people clamoring around two hucksters' carts. They were bidding their farthings and ha'pennies for a vegetable held up by the auctioneer, which he at last scornfully flung, with a gibe for its cheapness, to the successful bidder. In the momentary pause only one man detached himself from the groups. He had bidden in a cabbage, and when it struck his hand, he instantly sat down on the curb, tore it with his teeth, and hastily devoured it, unwashed and uncooked as it was. He and his fellows were types of the "submerged tenth," as our missionary guide told us, with some little satisfaction in the then new phrase, and he further added that so many of them could scarcely be seen in one spot save at this Saturday night auction, the desire for cheap food being apparently the one thing which could move them simultaneously. They were huddled into ill-fitting, cast-off clothing, the ragged finery which one sees only in East London. Their pale faces were dominated by that most unlovely of human expressions, the cunning and shrewdness of the bargain hunter who starves if he cannot make a successful trade, and yet the final impression was not of ragged, tawdry clothing nor of pinched and sallow faces, but of myriads of hands, empty, pathetic, nerveless, and work worn, showing white in the uncertain light of the street, and clutching forward for food which was already unfit to eat. . . .

. . . During the following two years on the continent, while I was irresistibly drawn to the poorer quarters of each city, nothing among the beggars of South Italy nor among the salt miners of Austria carried with it the same conviction of human wretchedness which was conveyed by this momentary glimpse of an East London street. It was, of course, a most fragmentary and lurid view of the poverty of East London, and quite unfair. I should have been shown either less or more, for I went away with no notion of the hundreds of men and women who had gallantly identified their fortunes with these empty-handed people, and who, in church and chapel, "relief works," and charities, were at least making an effort towards its mitigation. . . .

For two years in the midst of my distress over the poverty which, thus suddenly driven into my consciousness, had become to me the "Weltschmerz," there was mingled a sense of futility, of misdirected energy, the belief that the pursuit of cultivation would not in the end bring either solace or relief. I gradually reached a conviction that the first generation of college women had taken their learning too quickly, had departed too suddenly from the active, emotional life led by their grandmothers and great-grandmothers. . . .

In the German and French *pensions*, which twenty-five years ago were crowded with American mothers and their daughters who had crossed the seas in search of culture, one often found the mother making real connection with the life about her, using her inadequate German with great fluency, gaily measuring the enormous sheets or exchanging recipes with the German Hausfrau, visiting impartially the nearest kindergarten and market, making an atmosphere of her own, hearty and genuine as far as it went, in the house and on the street. On the other hand, her daughter was critical and uncertain of her linguistic acquirements, and only at ease when in the familiar receptive attitude afforded by the art gallery and opera house. . . .

I remember a happy busy mother who, complacent with the knowledge that her daughter daily devoted four hours to her music, looked up from her knitting to say, "If I had had your opportunities when I was young, my dear, I should have been a very happy girl. . . ."

. . . The girl looked wistfully at her mother, but had not the courage to cry out what was in her heart. . . . "You do not know what life means when all the difficulties are removed! I am simply smothered and sickened with advantages. It is like eating a sweet dessert the first thing in the morning."

This, then, was the difficulty, this sweet dessert in the morning and the assumption that the sheltered, educated girl has nothing to do with the bitter poverty and the social maladjustment which is all about her, and which, after all, cannot be concealed, for it breaks through poetry and literature in a burning tide which overwhelms her; it peers at her in the form of heavy-laden market women and underpaid street laborers, gibing her with a sense of her uselessness.

I recall one snowy morning in Saxe-Coburg, looking from the window of our little hotel upon the town square, that we saw crossing and recrossing it a single file of women with semicircular, heavy, wooden tanks fastened upon their backs. They were carrying in this primitive fashion to a remote cooling room these tanks filled with a hot brew incident to one stage of beer making. The women were bent forward, not only under the weight which they were bearing, but because the tanks were so high that it would have been impossible for them to have lifted their heads. Their faces and hands, reddened in the cold morning air, showed clearly the white scars where they had previously been scalded by the hot stuff which splashed if they stumbled ever so little on their way. Stung into action by one of those sudden indignations against cruel conditions which at times fill the young with unexpected energy, I found myself across the square . . . interviewing the phlegmatic owner of the brewery who received . . . me . . . with exasperating indifference. . . . I went back to a breakfast for which I had lost my appetite, as I had for Gray's *Life of Prince Albert* and his wonderful tutor, Baron Stockmar, which I had been reading late the night before. . . .

The wonder and beauty of Italy later brought healing and some relief to the paralyzing sense of the futility of all artistic and intellectual effort when disconnected from the ultimate test of the conduct it inspired. . . . I returned to Europe two years later in order to spend a winter in Rome . . . and to carry out a great desire to systematically study the Catacombs. In spite of my distrust of "advantages" I was apparently not yet so cured but that I wanted more of them. . . .

Other . . . summers were spent in the old home in northern Illinois, and one Sunday morning I received the rite of baptism and became a member of the Presbyterian church in the village. At this time there was certainly no outside pressure pushing me towards such a decision, and at twenty-five one does not ordinarily take such a step from a mere desire to conform. While I was not conscious of any emotional "conversion," I took upon myself the outward expressions of the religious life with all humility and sincerity. It was doubtless true that I was "Weary of myself and sick of asking / What I am and what I ought to be," and that various cherished safeguards and claims to self-dependence had been broken into by many piteous failures. But certainly I had been brought to the conclusion that "sincerely to give up one's conceit or hope of being good in one's own right is the only door to the Universe's deeper reaches." Perhaps the young clergyman recognized this as the test of the Christian temper, at any rate he required little assent to dogma or miracle, and assured me that while both the ministry and the officers of his church were obliged to subscribe to doctrines of well-known severity, the faith required to the laity was almost early Christian in its simplicity. . . . There was also growing within me an almost passionate devotion to the ideals of democracy, and when in all history had these ideals been so thrillingly expressed as when the faith of the fisherman and the slave had been boldly opposed to the accepted moral belief that the well-being of a privileged few might justly be built upon the ignorance and sacrifice of the many? . . .

In one of the . . . summers between . . . European journeys I visited a western state where I had formerly invested a sum of money in mortgages. I was much horrified by the wretched conditions among the farmers, which had resulted from a long period of drought, and one forlorn picture was fairly burned into my mind. A number of starved hogs—collateral for a promissory note—were huddled into an open pen. Their backs were humped in a curious, camel-like fashion, and they were devouring one of their own number, the latest victim of absolute starvation or possibly merely the one least able to defend himself against their voracious hunger. The farmer's wife looked on indifferently, a picture of despair as she stood in the door of the bare, crude house, and the two children behind her, whom she vainly tried to keep out of sight, continually thrust forward their faces almost covered by masses of coarse, sunburned hair, and their little bare feet so black, so hard, the great cracks so filled with dust that they looked like flattened hoofs. The children could not be compared to anything so joyous as satyrs, although they appeared but half-human. It seemed to me quite impossible to receive interest from mortgages placed upon farms which might at any season be reduced to such conditions, and with great inconvenience to my agent and doubtless with hardship to the farmers, as speedily as possible I withdrew all my investment. But something had to be done with the money, and in my reaction against unseen horrors I bought a farm near my native village and also a flock of innocent-looking sheep. My partner in the enterprise had not chosen the shepherd's lot as a permanent occupation, but hoped to speedily finish his college course upon half the proceeds of our venture. This pastoral enterprise still seems to me to have been essentially sound, both economically and morally, but perhaps one partner depended too much upon the impeccability of her motives and the other found himself too preoccupied with study to know that it is not a real kindness to bed a sheepfold with straw, for certainly the venture ended in a spectacle scarcely less harrowing than the memory it was designed to obliterate. At least the sight of two hundred sheep with four rotting hoofs each was not reassuring to one whose conscience craved economic peace. A fortunate series of sales of mutton, wool, and farm enabled the partners to end the enterprise without loss, and they passed on, one to college and the other to Europe, if not wiser, certainly sadder for the experience. . . .

The beginning of 1887 found me in a . . . little party of three in very picturesque lodgings in Rome, and settled into a certain student's routine. But my study of the Catacombs was brought to an abrupt end in a fortnight by a severe attack of sciatic rheumatism, which kept me in Rome with a trained nurse during many weeks, and later sent me to the Riviera to lead an invalid's life once more. . . .

It is hard to tell just when the very simple plan which afterward developed into the Settlement began to form itself in my mind. It may have been even before I went to Europe for the second time, but I gradually became convinced that it would be a good thing to rent a house in a part of the city where many primitive and actual needs are found, in which young women who had been given over too exclusively to study might restore a balance of activity along traditional lines and learn of life from life itself. . . .

. . . I can well recall the stumbling and uncertainty with which I finally set this plan . . . forth to Miss Starr, my old-time school friend . . . I even dared to hope that she might join in carrying it out. . . .

A month later we parted in Paris, Miss Starr to go back to Italy, and I to journey on to London to secure as many suggestions as possible from those wonderful places of which we had heard, Toynbee Hall and the People's Palace. So that it finally came about that in June 1888, five years after my first visit in East London, I found myself at Toynbee Hall equipped not only with a letter of introduction from Canon Fremantle, but with high expectations and a certain belief that whatever perplexities and discouragement concerning the life of the poor were in store for me, I should at least know something at first hand and have the solace of daily activity. I had confidence that although life itself might contain many difficulties, the period of mere passive receptivity had come to an end, and I had at last finished with the everlasting "preparation for life," however ill prepared I might be. . . .

Chapter Five

First Days at Hull House

THE NEXT JANUARY found Miss Starr and myself in Chicago, searching for a neighborhood in which we might put our plans into execution. In our eagerness to win friends for the new undertaking, we utilized every opportunity to set forth the meaning of the Settlement as it had been embodied at Toynbee Hall, although in those days we made no appeal for money, meaning to start with our own slender resources. . . .

In our search for a vicinity in which to settle we went about with the officers of the compulsory education department, with city missionaries, and with . . . newspaper reporters. . . .

One . . . Sunday afternoon in the early spring, on the way to a Bohemian mission in the carriage of one of its founders, we passed a fine old house standing well back from the street, surrounded on three sides by a broad piazza, which was supported by wooden pillars of exceptionally pure Corinthian design and proportion. I was so attracted by the house that I set forth to visit it the very next day, but though I searched for it then and for several days after, I could not find it, and at length I most reluctantly gave up the search.

Three weeks later, with the advice of several of the oldest residents of Chicago, including the ex-mayor of the city, Colonel Mason, who had from the first been a warm friend to our plans, we decided upon a location somewhere near the junction of Blue Island Avenue, Halsted Street, and Harrison Street. I was surprised and overjoyed on the very first day of our search for quarters to come upon the hospitable old house, the quest for which I had so recently abandoned. The house was of course rented, the lower part of it used for offices and storerooms in connection with a factory that stood back of it. However, after some difficulties were overcome, it proved to be possible to sublet the second floor and what had been a large drawing room on the first floor.

The house had passed through many changes since it had been built in 1856 for the homestead of one of Chicago's pioneer citizens, Mr. Charles J. Hull, and although battered by its vicissitudes, was essentially sound. Before it had been occupied by the factory, it had sheltered a secondhand furniture store, and at one time the Little Sisters of the Poor had used it for a home for the aged. . . .

The fine old house responded kindly to repairs, its wide hall and open fireplace always insuring it a gracious aspect. Its generous owner, Miss Helen Culver, in the following spring gave us a free leasehold of the entire house. Her kindness has continued through the years until the group of thirteen buildings, which at present comprises our equipment, is built largely upon land which Miss Culver has put at the service of the Settlement which bears Mr. Hull's name. In those days the house stood between an undertaking establishment and a saloon. "Knight, Death, and the Devil," the three were called by a Chicago wit, and yet any mock heroics which might be implied by comparing the Settlement to a knight quickly dropped away under the genuine kindness and hearty welcome extended to us by the families living up and down the street. . . .

On the 18th of September 1889, Miss Starr and I moved into it, with Miss Mary Keyser, who began performing the housework, but who quickly developed into a very important factor in the life of the vicinity as well as that of the household. . . .

Halsted Street has grown so familiar during twenty years of residence that it is difficult to recall its gradual changes—the withdrawal of the more prosperous Irish and Germans, and the slow substitution of Russian Jews, Italians, and Greeks. A description of the street such as I gave in those early addresses still stands in my mind as sympathetic and correct.

> . . . Between Halsted Street and the river live about ten thousand Italians—Neapolitans, Sicilians, and Calabrians, with an occasional Lombard or Venetian. To the south on Twelfth Street are many Germans and side streets are given over almost entirely to Polish and Russian Jews. Still farther south, these Jewish colonies merge into a huge Bohemian colony, so vast that Chicago ranks as the third Bohemian city in the world. To the northwest are many Canadian French, clannish in spite of their long residence in America, and to the north are Irish and first-generation Americans. On the streets directly west and farther north are well-to-do English speaking families, many of whom own their own houses and have lived in the neighborhood for years; one man is still living in his old farmhouse.

> The policy of the public authorities of never taking an initiative, and always waiting to be urged to do their duty, is obviously fatal in a neighborhood where there is little

initiative among the citizens. The idea underlying our self-government breaks down in such a ward. The streets are inexpressibly dirty, the number of schools inadequate, sanitary legislation unenforced, the street lighting bad, the paving miserable and altogether lacking in the alleys and smaller streets, and the stables foul beyond description. Hundreds of houses are unconnected with the street sewer. The older and richer inhabitants seem anxious to move away as rapidly as they can afford it. They make room for newly arrived immigrants who are densely ignorant of civic duties. This substitution of the older inhabitants is accomplished industrially also, in the south and east quarters of the ward. The Jews and Italians do the finishing for the great clothing manufacturers, formerly done by Americans, Irish, and Germans, who refused to submit to the extremely low prices to which the sweating system has reduced their successors. As the design of the sweating system is the elimination of rent from the manufacture of clothing, the "outside work" is begun after the clothing leaves the cutter. An unscrupulous contractor regards no basement as too dark, no stable loft too foul, no rear shanty too provisional, no tenement room too small for his workroom, as these conditions imply low rental. Hence these shops abound in the worst of the foreign districts where the sweater easily finds his cheap basement and his home finishers.

. . . Rear tenements flourish; many houses have no water supply save the faucet in the back yard, there are no fire escapes, the garbage and ashes are placed in wooden boxes which are fastened to the street pavements. One of the most discouraging features about the present system of tenement houses is that many are owned by sordid and ignorant immigrants. The theory that wealth brings responsibility, that possession entails at length education and refinement, in these cases fails utterly. . . .

In the very first weeks of our residence Miss Starr started a reading party in George Eliot's *Romola*, which was attended by a group of young women who followed the wonderful tale with unflagging interest. The weekly reading was held in our little upstairs dining room, and two members of the club came to dinner each week, not only that they might be received as guests, but that they might help us wash the dishes afterward. . . .

Volunteers to the new undertaking came quickly; a charming young girl conducted a kindergarten in the drawing room, coming regularly every morning from her home in a distant part of the North Side of the city. Although a tablet to her memory has stood upon a mantel shelf in Hull House for five years, we still associate her most vividly with the play of little children, first in her kindergarten and then in her own nursery, which furnished a veritable illustration of Victor Hugo's definition of heaven—"a place where parents are always young and children always little." Her daily presence for the first two years made it quite impossible for us to become too solemn and self-conscious in our strenuous routine, for her mirth and buoyancy were irresistible and her eager desire to share the life of the neighborhood never failed, although it was often put to a severe test. One day at luncheon she gaily recited her futile attempt to impress temperance principles upon the mind of an Italian mother, to whom she had returned a small daughter of five sent to the kindergarten "in quite a horrid state of intoxication" from the wine-soaked bread upon which she had breakfasted. The mother, with the gentle courtesy of a South Italian, listened politely to her graphic portrayal of the untimely end awaiting so immature a wine bibber; but long before the lecture was finished, quite unconscious of the incongruity, she hospitably set forth her best wines, and when her baffled guest refused one after the other, she disappeared, only to quickly return with a small dark glass of whisky, saying reassuringly, "See, I have brought you the true American drink." The recital ended in seriocomic despair, with the rueful statement that "the impression I probably made on her darkened mind was, that it was the American custom to breakfast children on bread soaked in whisky instead of light Italian wine."

That first kindergarten was a constant source of education to us. We were much surprised to find social distinctions even among its lambs, although greatly amused with the neat formulation made by the superior little Italian boy who refused to sit beside uncouth little Angelina because "we eat our macaroni this way"—imitating the movement of a fork from a plate to his mouth—"and she eat her macaroni this way," holding his hand high in the air and throwing back his head, that his wide-open mouth might receive an imaginary cascade. Angelina gravely nodded her little head in approval of this distinction between gentry and peasant. . . .

The dozens of younger children who from the first came to Hull House were organized into groups which were not quite classes and not quite clubs. The value of these groups consisted almost entirely in arousing a higher imagination and in giving the children the opportunity which they could not have in the crowded schools, for initiative and for independent social relationships. The public schools then contained little handwork of any sort, so that naturally any instruction which we provided for the children took the direction of this supplementary work. But it required a constant effort that the pressure of poverty itself should not defeat the educational aim. The Italian girls in the sewing classes would count the day lost when they could not carry home a garment, and the insistence that it should be neatly made seemed a super-refinement to those in dire need of clothing.

As these clubs have been continued during the twenty years they have developed classes in the many forms of handicraft which the newer education is so rapidly adapting for the delight of children; but they still keep their essentially social character and still minister to that large number of children who leave school the very week they are fourteen years old, only too eager to close the schoolroom door forever on a tiresome task that is at last well over. It seems to us important that these children shall find themselves permanently attached to a House that offers them evening clubs and classes with their old companions, that merges as easily as possible the school life into the working life and does what it can to find places for the bewildered young things looking for work. A large proportion of the delinquent boys brought into the juvenile court in Chicago are the oldest sons in large families whose wages are needed at home. The grades from which many of them leave school, as the records show, are piteously far from the seventh and eighth where the very first introduction in manual training is given, nor have they been caught by any other abiding interest.

In spite of these flourishing clubs for children early established at Hull House, and the fact that our first organized undertaking was a kindergarten, we were very insistent that the Settlement should not be primarily for the children, and that it was absurd to suppose that grown people would not respond to opportunities for education and social life. Our enthusiastic kindergartner herself demonstrated this with an old woman of ninety who, because she was left alone all day while her daughter cooked in a restaurant, had formed such a persistent habit of picking the plaster off the walls that one landlord after another refused to have her for a tenant. It required but a few week's time to teach her to make large paper chains, and gradually she was content to do it all day long, and in the end took quite as much pleasure in adorning the walls as she had formally taken in demolishing them. Fortunately the landlord had never heard the aesthetic principle that exposure of basic construction is more desirable than gaudy decoration. In course of time it was discovered that the old woman could speak Gaelic, and when one or two grave professors came to see her, the neighborhood was filled with pride that such a wonder lived in their midst. To mitigate life for a woman of ninety was an unfailing refutation of the statement that the Settlement was designed for the young. . . .

In those early days we were often asked why we had come to live on Halsted Street when we could afford to live somewhere else. I remember one man who used to shake his head and say it was "the strangest thing he had met in his experience," but who was finally convinced that it was "not strange but natural." In time it came to seem natural to all of us that the Settlement should be there. If it is natural to feed the hungry and care for the sick, it is certainly natural to give pleasure to the young, comfort to the aged, and to minister to the deep-seated craving for social intercourse that all men feel. . . .

From the first it seemed understood that we were ready to perform the humblest neighborhood services. We were asked to wash the newborn babies, and to prepare the dead for burial, to nurse the sick, and to "mind the children."

Occasionally these neighborly offices unexpectedly uncovered ugly human traits. For six weeks after an operation we kept in one of our three bedrooms a forlorn little baby who, because he was born with a cleft palate, was most unwelcome even to his mother, and we were horrified when he died of neglect a week after he was returned to his home; a little Italian bride of fifteen sought shelter with us one November evening to escape her husband who had beaten her every night for a week when he returned home from work, because she had lost her wedding ring; two of us officiated quite alone at the birth of an illegitimate child because the doctor was late in arriving, and none of the honest Irish matrons would "touch the likes of her"; we ministered at the deathbed of a young man, who during a long illness of tuberculosis had received so many bottles of whisky through the mistaken kindness of his friends, that the cumulative effect produced wild periods of exultation, in one of which he died. . . .

But in spite of some untoward experiences, we were constantly impressed with the uniform kindness and courtesy we received. Perhaps these first days laid the simple human foundations which are certainly essential for continuous living among the poor; first, genuine preference for residence in an industrial quarter to any other part of the city, because it is interesting and makes the human appeal; and second, the conviction, in the words of Canon Barnett, that the things that make men alike are finer and better than the things that keep them apart, and that these basic likenesses, if they are properly accentuated, easily transcend the less essential differences of race, language, creed, and tradition.

Perhaps even in those first days we made a beginning toward that object which was afterwards stated in our charter:

To provide a center for a higher civic and
social life; to institute and maintain educational and philanthropic enterprises, and
to investigate and improve the conditions
in the industrial districts of Chicago.

Chapter Seven

Some Early Undertakings at Hull House

IF THE EARLY American Settlements stood for a more exigent standard in philanthropic activities, insisting that each new undertaking should be preceded by carefully ascertained facts, then certainly Hull House held to this standard in the opening of our new coffeehouse first started as a public kitchen. An investigation of the sweatshops had disclosed the fact that sewing women during the busy season paid little attention to the feeding of their families, for it was only by working steadily through the long day that the scanty pay of five, seven, or nine cents for finishing a dozen pairs of trousers could be made into a day's wage; and they bought from the nearest grocery the canned goods that could be most quickly heated, or gave a few pennies to the children with which they might secure a lunch from a neighboring candy shop.

One of the residents made an investigation, at the instance of the United States Department of Agriculture, into the food values of the dietaries of the various immigrants, and this was followed by an investigation made by another resident, for the United States Department of Labor, into the foods of the Italian colony, on the supposition that the constant use of imported products bore a distinct relation to the cost of living. I recall an Italian who, coming into Hull House one day as we were sitting at the dinner table, expressed great surprise that Americans ate a variety of food, because he believed that they partook only of potatoes and beer. A little inquiry showed that this conclusion was drawn from the fact that he lived next to an Irish saloon and had never seen anything but potatoes going in and beer coming out.

At that time the New England kitchen was comparatively new in Boston, and Mrs. Richards, who was largely responsible for its foundation, hoped that cheaper cuts of meat and simpler vegetables, if they were subjected to slow and thorough processes of cooking, might be made attractive and their nutritive value secured for the people who so sadly needed more nutritious food. It was felt that this could be best accomplished in public kitchens, where the advantage of scientific training and careful supervision could be secured. One of the residents went to Boston for a training under Mrs. Richards, and when the Hull House kitchen was fitted under her guidance and direction, our hopes ran high for some modification of the food of the neighborhood. We did not reckon, however, with the wide diversity in nationality and inherited tastes, and while we sold a certain amount of the carefully prepared soups and stews in the neighboring factories—a sale which has steadily increased throughout the years—and were also patronized by a few households, perhaps the neighborhood estimate was best summed up by the woman who frankly confessed, that the food was certainly nutritious, but that she didn't like to eat what was nutritious, that she liked to eat "what she'd ruther."

If the dietetics were appreciated but slowly, the social value of the coffeehouse and the gymnasium, which were in the same building, were quickly demonstrated. At that time the saloon halls were the only places in the neighborhood where the immigrant could hold his social gatherings, and where he could celebrate such innocent and legitimate occasions as weddings and christenings.

These halls were rented very cheaply with the understanding that various sums of money should be "passed across the bar," and it was considered a mean host or guest who failed to live up to this implied bargain. The consequence was that many a reputable party ended with a certain amount of disorder, due solely to the fact that the social instinct was traded upon and used as a basis for moneymaking by an adroit host. From the beginning the young people's clubs had asked for dancing, and nothing was more popular than the increased space for parties offered by the gymnasium, with the chance to serve refreshments in the room below. We tried experiments with every known "soft drink," from those extracted from an expensive soda water fountain to slender glasses of grape juice, but so far as drinks were concerned we never became a rival to the saloon, nor indeed did anyone imagine that we were trying to do so. I remember one man who looked about the cozy little room and said, "This would be a nice place to sit in all day if one could only have beer." But the coffeehouse gradually performed a mission of its own and became something of a social center to the neighborhood as well as a real convenience. Businessmen from the adjacent factories and schoolteachers from the nearest public schools used it increasingly. The Hull House students and club members supped together in little groups or held their reunions and social banquets, as, to a certain extent, did organizations from all parts of the town. The experience of the coffeehouse taught us not to hold to preconceived ideas of what the neighborhood ought to have, but to keep ourselves in readiness to modify and adapt our undertakings as we discovered those things which the neighborhood was ready to accept.

Better food was doubtless needed, but more attractive and safer places for social gatherings were also needed, and the neighborhood was ready for one and not for the other. We had no hint then in Chicago of the small parks which were to be established fifteen years later, containing the halls for dancing and their own restaurants in buildings where the natural desire of the young for gaiety and social organization, could be safely indulged. Yet even in that early day a member of the Hull House Men's Club who had been appointed superintendent of Douglas Park had secured there the first public swimming pool, and his fellow club members were proud of the achievement. . . .

Of course there was always present the harrowing consciousness of the difference in economic condition between ourselves and our neighbors. Even if we had gone to live in the most wretched tenement, there would have always been an essential difference between them and ourselves, for we should have had a sense of security in regard to illness and old age and the lack of these two securities are the specters which most persistently haunt the poor. Could we, in spite of this, make their individual efforts more effective through organization and possibly complement them by small efforts of our own?

Some such vague hope was in our minds when we started the Hull House Cooperative Coal Association, which led a vigorous life for three years, and developed a large membership under the skillful advice of its one paid officer, an English workingman who had had experience in cooperative societies at "'ome." Some of the meetings of the association, in which people met to consider together their basic dependence upon fire and warmth, had a curious challenge of life about them. Because the cooperators knew what it meant to bring forth children in the midst of privation and to see the tiny creatures struggle for life, their recitals cut a cross section, as it were, in that world-old effort—the "dying to live" which so inevitably triumphs over poverty and suffering. And yet their very familiarity with hardship may have been responsible for that sentiment which traditionally ruins business, for a vote of the cooperators that the basket buyers be given one basket free out of every six, that the presentation of five purchase tickets should entitle the holders to a profit in coal instead of stock "because it would be a shame to keep them waiting for the dividend," was always pointed to by the conservative quarter-of-a-ton buyers as the beginning of the end. At any rate, at the close of the third winter, although the Association occupied an imposing coal yard on the southeast corner of the Hull House block and its gross receipts were between three and four hundred dollars a day, it became evident that the concern could not remain solvent if it continued its philanthropic policy, and the experiment was terminated by the cooperators taking up their stock in the remaining coal.

Our next cooperative experiment was much more successful, perhaps because it was much more spontaneous.

At a meeting of working girls held at Hull House during a strike in a large shoe factory, the discussions made it clear that the strikers who had been most easily frightened, and therefore first to capitulate, were naturally those girls who were paying board and were afraid of being put out if they fell too far behind. After a recital of a case of peculiar hardship one of them exclaimed: "Wouldn't it be fine if we had a boarding club of our own, and then we could stand by each other in a time like this?" After that events moved quickly. We read aloud together Beatrice Potter's little book on "Cooperation," and discussed all the difficulties and fascinations of such an undertaking, and on the first of May 1891, two comfortable apartments near Hull House were rented and furnished. The Settlement was responsible for the furniture and paid the first month's rent, but beyond that the members managed the club themselves. The undertaking "marched," as the French say, from the very first, and always on its own feet. Although there were difficulties, none of them proved insurmountable, which was a matter for great satisfaction in the face of a statement made by the head of the United States Department of Labor, who, on a visit to the club when it was but two years old, said that his department had investigated many cooperative undertakings, and that none founded and managed by women had ever succeeded. At the end of the third year the club occupied all of the six apartments which the original building contained, and numbered fifty members.

It was in connection with our efforts to secure a building for the Jane Club, that we first found ourselves in the dilemma between the needs of our neighbors and the kind-hearted response upon which we had already come to rely for their relief. The adapted apartments in which the Jane Club was housed were inevitably more or less uncomfortable, and we felt that the success of the club justified the erection of a building for its sole use.

Up to that time, our history had been as the minor peace of the early Church. We had had the most generous interpretation of our efforts. Of course, many people were indifferent to the idea of the Settlement; others looked on with tolerant and sometimes cynical amusement which we would often encounter in a good story related at our expense; but all this was remote and unreal to us, and we were sure that if the critics could but touch "the life of the people," they would understand.

The situation changed markedly after the Pullman strike, and our efforts to secure factory legislation later brought upon us a certain amount of distrust and suspicion; until then we had been considered merely a kindly philanthropic undertaking whose new form gave us a certain idealistic glamour. But sterner tests were coming, and one of the first was in connection with the new building for the Jane Club. A trustee of Hull House came to see us one day with the good news that a friend of his was ready to give twenty thousand dollars with which to build the desired new clubhouse. When, however, he divulged the name of his generous friend, it proved to be that of a man who was notorious for underpaying the girls in his establishment and concerning whom there were even darker stories. It seemed clearly impossible to erect a clubhouse for working girls with such money and we at once said that we must decline the offer. The trustee of Hull House was put in the most embarrassing situation; he had, of course, induced the man to give the money and had had no thought but that it would be eagerly received; he would now be obliged to return with the astonishing, not to say insulting, news that the money was considered unfit.

In the long discussion which followed, it gradually became clear to all of us that such a refusal could be valuable only as it might reveal to the man himself and to others, public opinion in regard to certain methods of moneymaking, but that from the very nature of the case our refusal of this money could not be made public because a representative of Hull House had asked for it. However, the basic fact remained that we could not accept the money, and of this the trustee himself was fully convinced. This incident occurred during a period of much discussion concerning "tainted money" and is perhaps typical of the difficulty of dealing with it. It is impossible to know how far we may blame the individual for doing that which all of his competitors and his associates consider legitimate; at the same time, social changes can only be inaugurated by those who feel the unrighteousness of contemporary conditions, and the expression of their scruples may be the one opportunity for pushing forward moral tests into that dubious area wherein wealth is accumulated.

In the course of time a new clubhouse was built by an old friend of Hull House much interested in working girls, and this has been occupied for twelve years by the very successful cooperating Jane Club. . . .

There was room for discouragement in the many unsuccessful experiments in cooperation which were carried on in Chicago during the early nineties; a carpenter shop on Van Buren Street near Halsted, a labor exchange started by the unemployed, not so paradoxical an arrangement as it seems, and a very ambitious plan for a country colony which was finally carried out at Ruskin, Tennessee. In spite of failures, cooperative schemes went on, some of the same men appearing in one after another with irrepressible optimism. . . .

. . . One's faith is kept alive as one occasionally meets a realized ideal of better human relations. At least traces of successful cooperation are found even in individualistic America. I recall my enthusiasm on the day when I set forth to lecture at New Harmony, Indiana, for I had early been thrilled by the tale of Robert Owen, as every young person must be who is interested in social reform; I was delighted to find so much of his spirit still clinging to the little town which had long ago held one of his ardent experiments, although the poor old cooperators, who for many years claimed friendship at Hull House because they heard that we "had once tried a cooperative coal association," might well have convinced me of the persistency of the cooperative ideal.

Many experiences in those early years, although vivid, seemed to contain no illumination; nevertheless they doubtless permanently affected our judgments concerning what is called crime and vice. . . .

I recall our perplexity over the first girls who had "gone astray"—the poor, little, forlorn objects, fifteen and sixteen years old, with their moral natures apparently untouched and unawakened; one of them whom the police had found in a professional house and asked us to shelter for a few days until she could be used as a witness, was clutching a battered doll which she had kept with her during her six months of an "evil life." Two of these prematurely aged children came to us one day directly from the maternity ward of the Cook County hospital, each with a baby in her arms, asking for protection, because they did not want to go home for fear of "being licked. . . ."

But discouraging as these and other similar efforts often were, nevertheless the difficulties were infinitely less in those days when we dealt with "fallen girls" than in the years following when the "white slave traffic" became gradually established and when agonized parents, as well as the victims themselves, were totally unable to account for the situation. In the light of recent disclosures, it seems as if we were unaccountably dull not to have seen what was happening, especially to the Jewish girls among whom "the home trade of the white slave traffic" was first carried on and who were thus made to break through countless generations of chastity. We early encountered the difficulties of that old problem of restoring the woman, or even the child, into the society she has once outraged. I well remember our perplexity when we attempted to help two girls straight from a Virginia tobacco factory, who had been decoyed into a disreputable house when innocently seeking a lodging on the late evening of their arrival. Although they had been rescued promptly, the stigma remained, and we found it impossible to permit them to join any of the social clubs connected with Hull House, not so much because there was danger of contamination, as because the parents of the club members would have resented their presence most hotly. One of our trustees succeeded in persuading a repentant girl, fourteen years old, whom we tried to give a fresh start in another part of the city, to attend a Sunday School class of a large Chicago church. The trustee hoped that the contact with nice girls, as well as the moral training, would help the poor child on her hard road. But unfortunately tales of her shortcomings reached the superintendent who felt obliged, in order to protect the other girls, to forbid her the school. She came back to tell us about it, defiant as well as discouraged, and had it not been for the experience with our own clubs, we could easily have joined her indignation over a church which "acted as if its Sunday School was a show window for candy kids."

In spite of poignant experiences or, perhaps, because of them, the memory of the first years at Hull House is more or less blurred with fatigue, for we could of course become accustomed only gradually to the unending activity and to the confusion of a house constantly filling and refilling with groups of people. The little children who came to the kindergarten in the morning were followed by the afternoon clubs of older children, and those in turn made way for the educational and social organizations of adults, occupying every room in the house every evening. All one's habits of living had to be readjusted, and any student's tendency to sit with a book by the fire was of necessity definitely abandoned. . . .

. . . We built new buildings which were very precious to us and it afforded us the greatest pride and pleasure as one building after another was added to the Hull House group. They clothed in brick and mortar and made visible to the world that which we were trying to do; they stated to Chicago that education and recreation ought to be extended to the immigrants. The boys came in great numbers to our provisional gymnasium fitted up in a former saloon, and it seemed to us quite as natural that a Chicago man, fond of athletics, should erect a building for them, as that the boys should clamor for more room.

I do not wish to give a false impression, for we were often bitterly pressed for money and worried by the prospect of unpaid bills, and we gave up one golden scheme after another because we could not afford it; we cooked the meals and kept the books and washed the windows without a thought of hardship if we thereby saved money for the consummation of some ardently desired undertaking.

. . . A house in which the men residents lived was opened across the street, and at the end of the first five years the Hull House residential force numbered fifteen, a majority of whom still remain identified with the Settlement. . . .

Occasionally I obscurely felt as if a demand were being made upon us for a ritual which should express and carry forward the hope of the social movement. I was constantly bewildered by the number of requests I received to officiate at funeral services and by the curious confessions made to me by total strangers. For a time I accepted the former and on one awful occasion furnished "the poetic part" of a wedding ceremony really performed by a justice of the peace, but I soon learned to steadfastly refuse such offices, although I saw that for many people without church affiliations the vague humanitarianism the Settlement represented was the nearest approach they could find to an expression of their religious sentiments. . . .

In those early years at Hull House we were . . . in no danger of losing ourselves in mazes of speculation or mysticism, and there was shrewd penetration in a compliment I received from one of our Scotch neighbors. He came down Polk Street as I was standing near the foundations of our new gymnasium, and in response to his friendly remark that "Hull House was spreading out," I replied that "Perhaps we were spreading out too fast." "Oh, no," he rejoined, "you can afford to spread out wide, you are so well planted in the mud," giving the compliment, however, a practical turn, as he glanced at the deep mire on the then unpaved street. It was this same condition of Polk Street which had caused the crown prince of Belgium when he was brought upon a visit to Hull House to shake his head and meditatively remark, "There is not such a street—no, not one—in all the territory of Belgium."

At the end of five years the residents of Hull House published some first found facts and our reflections thereon in a book called *Hull House Maps and Papers*. The maps were taken from information collected by one of the residents for the United States Bureau of Labor in the investigation into "the slums of great cities" and the papers treated of various neighborhood matters with candor and genuine concern if not with skill. The first edition became exhausted in two years, and apparently the Boston publisher did not consider the book worthy of a second.

Chapter Eight
Problems of Poverty

THAT NEGLECTED AND forlorn old age is daily brought to the attention of a Settlement which undertakes to bear its share of the neighborhood burden imposed by poverty, was pathetically clear to us during our first months of residence at Hull House. One day a boy of ten led a tottering old lady into the House, saying that she had slept for six weeks in their kitchen on a bed made up next to the stove; that she had come when her son died, although none of them had ever seen her before; but because her son had "once worked in the same shop with Pa she thought of him when she had nowhere to go." The little fellow concluded by saying that our house was so much bigger than theirs that he thought we would have more room for beds. The old woman herself said absolutely nothing, but looking on with that gripping fear of the poorhouse in her eyes, she was a living embodiment of that dread which is so heartbreaking that the occupants of the County Infirmary themselves seem scarcely less wretched than those who are making their last stand against it.

This look was almost more than I could bear for only a few days before some frightened women had bidden me come quickly to the house of an old German woman, whom two men from the country agent's office were attempting to remove to the County Infirmary. The poor old creature had thrown herself bodily upon a small and battered chest of drawers and clung there, clutching it so firmly that it would have been impossible to remove her without also taking the piece of furniture. She did not weep nor moan nor indeed make any human sound, but between her broken gasps for breath she squealed shrilly like a frightened animal caught in a trap. The little group of women and children gathered at her door stood aghast at this realization of the black dread which always clouds the lives of the very poor when work is slack, but which constantly grows more imminent and threatening as old age approaches. The neighborhood women and I hastened to make all sorts of promises as to the support of the old woman and the country officials, only too glad to be rid of their unhappy duty, left her to our ministrations. . . .

The poor creature who clung so desperately to her chest of drawers was really clinging to the last remnant of normal living—a symbol of all she was asked to renounce. For several years after this summer I invited five or six old women to take a two weeks' vacation from the poorhouse which was eagerly and even gaily accepted. Almost all the old men in the County Infirmary wander away each summer taking their chances for finding food or shelter and return much refreshed by the little "tramp," but the old women cannot do this unless they have some help from the outside, and yet the expenditure of a very little money secures for them the coveted vacation. I found that a few pennies paid their car fare into town, a dollar a week procured lodging with an old acquaintance; assured of two good meals a day in the Hull House coffeehouse they could count upon numerous cups of tea among old friends to whom they would airily state that they had "come out for a little change" and hadn't yet made up their minds about "going in again for the winter." They thus enjoyed a two weeks' vacation to the top of their bent and returned with wondrous tales of their adventures, with which they regaled the other paupers during the long winter. . . .

As social reformers gave themselves over to discussion of general principles, so the poor invariably accused poverty itself of their destruction. I recall a certain Mrs. Moran, who was returning one rainy day from the office of the county agent with her arms full of paper bags containing beans and flour which alone lay between her children and starvation. Although she had no money she boarded a street car in order to save her booty from complete destruction by the rain, and as the burst bags dropped "flour on the ladies' dresses" and "beans all over the place," she was sharply reprimanded by the conductor, who was the further exasperated when he discovered she had no fare. He put her off, as she had hoped he would, almost in front of Hull House. She related to us her state of mind as she stepped off the car and saw the last of her wares disappearing; she admitted she forgot the proprieties and "cursed a little," but, curiously enough, she pronounced her malediction, not against the rain nor the conductor, nor yet against the worthless husband who had been sent up to the city prison, but, true to the Chicago spirit of the moment, went to the root of the matter and roundly "cursed poverty."

This spirit of generalization and lack of organization among the charitable forces of the city was painfully revealed in that terrible winter after the World's Fair, when the general financial depression throughout the country was much intensified in Chicago by the numbers of unemployed stranded at the close of the exposition. When the first cold weather came the police stations and the very corridors of the city hall were crowded by men who could afford no other lodging. They made huge demonstrations on the lakefront, reminding one of the London gatherings in Trafalgar Square.

. . . Before Mr. Stead . . . published *If Christ Came to Chicago*, he made his attempt to rally the diverse moral forces of the city in a huge mass meeting, which resulted in a temporary organization, later developing into the Civic Federation. I was a member of the committee of five appointed to carry out the suggestions made in this remarkable meeting, and our first concern was to appoint a committee to deal with the unemployed. But when has a committee ever dealt satisfactorily with the unemployed? Relief stations were opened in various parts of the city, temporary lodging houses were established, Hull House undertaking to lodge the homeless women who could be received nowhere else; employment stations were opened giving sewing to the women, and street sweeping for the men was organized. It was in connection with the latter that the perplexing question of the danger of permanently lowering wages at such a crisis, in the praiseworthy effort to bring speedy relief, was brought home to me. I insisted that it was better to have the men work half a day for seventy-five cents than a whole day for a dollar, better that they should earn three dollars in two days than in three days. I resigned from the street-cleaning committee in despair of making the rest of the committee understand that, as our real object was not street cleaning but the help of the unemployed, we must treat the situation in such wise that the men would not be worse off when they returned to their normal occupations. . . .

A beginning also was then made toward a Bureau of Organized Charities, the main office being put in charge of a young man recently come from Boston, who lived at Hull House. But to employ scientific methods for the first time at such a moment involved difficulties, and the most painful episode of the winter came for me from an attempt on my part to conform to carefully received instructions. A shipping clerk whom I had known for a long time had lost his place, as so many people had that year, and came to the relief station established at Hull House four or five times to secure help for his family. I told him one day of the opportunity for work on the drainage canal and intimated that if any employment were obtainable, he ought to exhaust that possibility before asking for help. The man replied that he had always worked indoors and that he could not endure outside work in winter. I am grateful to remember that I was too uncertain to be severe, although I held to my instructions. He did not come again for relief, but worked for two days digging on the canal, where he contracted pneumonia and died a week later. I have never lost trace of the two little children he left behind him, although I cannot see them without a bitter consciousness that it was at their expense I learned that life cannot be administered by definite rules and regulations; that wisdom to deal with a man's difficulties comes only through some knowledge of his life and habits as a whole; and that to treat an isolated episode is almost sure to invite blundering.

It was also during this winter that I became permanently impressed with the kindness of the poor to each other; the woman who lives upstairs will willingly share her breakfast with the family below because she knows they "are hard up"; the man who boarded with them last winter will give a month's rent because he knows the father of the family is out of work; the baker across the street who is fast being pushed to the wall by his downtown competitors, will send across three loaves of stale bread because he has seen the children looking longingly into his window and suspects they are hungry. . . .

I remember one family in which the father had been out of work for this same winter, most of the furniture had been pawned, and as the worn-out shoes could not be replaced the children could not go to school. The mother was ill and barely able to come for the supplies and medicines. Two years later she invited me to supper one Sunday evening in the little home which had been completely restored, and she gave as a reason for the invitation that she couldn't bear to have me remember them as they had been during that one winter. . . .

We early found ourselves spending many hours in efforts to secure support for deserted women, insurance for bewildered widows, damages for injured operators, furniture from the clutches of the installment store. The Settlement is valuable as an information and interpretation bureau. It constantly acts between the various institutions of the city and the people for whose benefit these institutions were erected. The hospitals, the county agencies, and State asylums are often but vague rumors to the people who need them most. Another function of the Settlement to its neighborhood resembles that of the big brother whose mere presence on the playground protects the little one from bullies.

We early learned to know the children of hard-driven mothers who went out to work all day, sometimes leaving the little things in the casual care of a neighbor, but often locking them into their tenement rooms. The first three crippled children we encountered in the neighborhood had all been injured while their mothers were at work: one had fallen out of a third-story window, another had been burned, and the third had a curved spine due to the fact that for three years he had been tied all day long to the leg of the kitchen table, only released at noon by his older brother who hastily ran in from a neighboring factory to share his lunch with him. When the hot weather came the restless children could not brook the confinement of the stuffy rooms; and as it was not considered safe to leave the doors open because of sneak thieves, many of the children were locked out. During our first summer an increasing number of these poor little mites would wander into the cool hallway of Hull House. We kept them there and fed them at noon, in return for which we were sometimes offered a hot penny which had been held in a tight little fist "ever since mother left this morning, to buy something to eat with." Out of kindergarten hours our little guests noisily enjoyed the hospitality of our bedrooms under the so-called care of any resident who volunteered to keep an eye on them, but later they were moved into a neighboring apartment under more systematic supervision.

Hull House was thus committed to a day nursery which we sustained for sixteen years first in a little cottage on a side street and then in a building designed for its use called the Children's House. It is now carried on by the United Charities of Chicago in a finely equipped building on our block, where the immigrant mothers are cared for as well as the children. . . .

. . . I recall . . . the mother of "Goosie," as the children for years called a little boy who, because he was brought to the nursery wrapped up in his mother's shawl, always had his hair filled with the down and small feathers from the feather brush factory where she worked. One March morning, Goosie's mother was hanging out the washing on a shed roof before she left for the factory. Five-year-old Goosie was trotting at her heels handing her clothes pins, when he was suddenly blown off the roof by the high wind into the alley below. His neck was broken by the fall, and as he lay piteous and limp on a pile of frozen refuse, his mother cheerily called him to "climb up again," so confident do overworked mothers become that their children cannot get hurt. After the funeral, as the poor mother sat in the nursery postponing the moment when she must go back to her empty rooms, I asked her, in a futile effort to be of comfort, if there was anything more we could do for her. The overworked, sorrow-stricken woman looked up and replied, "If you could give me my wages for tomorrow, I would not go to work in the factory at all. I would like to stay at home all day and hold the baby. Goosie was always asking me to take him and I never had any time." This statement revealed the condition of many nursery mothers who are obliged to forego the joys and solaces which belong to even the most poverty-stricken. The long hours of factory labor necessary for earning the support of a child leave no time for the tender care and caressing which may enrich the life of the most piteous baby.

With all of the efforts made by modern society to nurture and educate the young, how stupid it is to permit the mothers of young children to spend themselves in the coarser work of the world! It is curiously inconsistent that with the emphasis which this generation has placed upon the mother and upon the prolongation of infancy, we constantly allow the waste of this most precious material. I cannot recall without indignation a recent experience. I was detained late one evening in an office building by a prolonged committee meeting of the Board of Education. As I came out at eleven o'clock, I met in the corridor of the fourteenth floor a woman whom I knew, on her knees scrubbing the marble tiling. As she straightened up to greet me, she seemed so wet from her feet up to her chin, that I hastily inquired the cause. Her reply was that she left home at five o'clock every night and had no opportunity for six hours to nurse her baby. Her mother's milk mingled with the very water with which she scrubbed the floors until she should return at midnight, heated and exhausted, to feed her screaming child with what remained within her breasts. . . .

Chapter Nine

A Decade of Economic Discussion

66 "THE WORKING PEOPLE'S Social Science Club" was organized at Hull House in the spring of 1890 by an English workingman, and for seven years it held a weekly meeting. At eight o'clock every Wednesday night the secretary called to order from forty to one hundred people; a chairman for the evening was elected, a speaker was introduced who was allowed to talk until nine o'clock; his subject was then thrown open to discussion and a lively debate ensued until ten o'clock, at which hour the meeting was declared adjourned. The enthusiasm of this club seldom lagged. Its zest for discussion was unceasing, and any attempt to turn it into a study or reading club always met with the strong disapprobation of the members. . . .

It was doubtless owing largely to this club that Hull House contracted its early reputation for radicalism. Visitors refused to distinguish between the sentiments expressed by its members in the heat of discussion and the opinions held by the residents themselves. At that moment in Chicago the radical of every shade of opinion was vigorous and dogmatic; of the sort that could not resign himself to the slow march of human improvement; of the type who knew exactly "in what part of the world Utopia standeth. . . ."

And yet as I recall the members of this early club, even those who talked the most and the least rationally, seem to me to have been particularly kindly and "safe." The most pronounced anarchist among them has long since become a convert to a religious sect, holding Buddhistic tenets which imply little food and a distrust of all action; he has become a wraith of his former self but he still retains his kindly smile. . . .

During those first years on Halsted Street nothing was more painfully clear than the fact that pliable human nature is relentlessly pressed upon by its physical environment. I saw nowhere a more devoted effort to understand and relieve that heavy pressure than the socialists were making, and I should have been glad to have had the comradeship of that gallant company had they not firmly insisted that fellowship depends upon identity of creed. They repudiated similarity of aim and social sympathy as tests which were much too loose and wavering as they did that vague socialism which for thousands has come to be a philosophy or rather religion embodying the hope of the world and the protection of all who suffer.

I also longed for the comfort of a definite social creed, which should afford at one and the same time an explanation of the social chaos and the logical steps towards its better ordering. . . . But another difficulty in the way of accepting this economic determinism, so baldly dependent upon the theory of class-consciousness, constantly arose when I lectured in country towns and there had opportunities to read human documents of prosperous people as well as those of my neighbors who were crowded into the city. The former were stoutly unconscious of any classes in America, and the class-consciousness of the immigrants was fast being broken into by the necessity for making new and unprecedented connections in the industrial life all about them. . . .

Trades unionists, unless they were also socialists, were not prominent in those economic discussions, although they were steadily making an effort to bring order into the unnecessary industrial confusion. They belonged to the second of the two classes into which Mill divides all those who are dissatisfied with human life as it is, and whose feelings are wholly identified with its radical amendment. He states that the thoughts of one class are in the region of ultimate aims, of "the highest ideals of human life," while the thoughts of the other are in the region of the "immediately useful and practically attainable." . . .

. . . There were certainly moments during the heated discussions of this decade when nothing seemed so important as right theory: this was borne in upon me one brilliant evening at Hull House when Benjamin Kidd, author of the much-read *Social Evolution*, was pitted against Victor Berger of Milwaukee, even then considered a rising man in the Socialist Party.

At any rate the residents of Hull House discovered that while their first impact with city poverty allied them to groups given over to discussion of social theories, their sober efforts to heal neighborhood ills allied them to general public movements which were without challenging creeds. But while we discovered that we most easily secured the smallest of much-needed improvements by attaching our efforts to those of organized bodies, nevertheless these very organizations would have been impossible, had not the public conscience been aroused and the community sensibility quickened by these same ardent theorists.

As I review these very first impressions of the workers in unskilled industries, living in a depressed quarter of the city, I realize how easy it was for us to see exceptional cases of hardship as typical of the average lot, and yet, in spite of alleviating philanthropy and labor legislation, the indictment of Tolstoy applied to Moscow thirty years ago still fits every American city:

> Wherever we may live, if we draw a circle around us of a hundred thousand, or a thousand, or even of ten miles circumference, and look at the lives of those men and women who are inside our circle, we shall find half-starved children, old people, pregnant women, sick and weak persons, working beyond their strength, who have neither food nor rest enough to support them, and who, for this reason, die before their time; we shall see others, full grown, who are injured and needlessly killed by dangerous and hurtful tasks. . . .

. . . Although the residents of Hull House were often baffled by the radicalism within the Social Science Club and harassed by the criticism from outside, we still continued to believe that such discussion should be carried on, for if the Settlement seeks its expression through social activity, it must learn the difference between mere social unrest and spiritual impulse.

The group of Hull House residents, which by the end of the decade comprised twenty-five, differed widely in social beliefs, from the girl direct from the country who looked upon all social unrest as mere anarchy, to the resident, who had become a socialist when a student in Zurich, and who had long before translated from the German Engel's *Conditions of the Working Class in England*, although at this time she had been read out of the Socialist Party because the Russian and German Impossibilists suspected her fluent English, as she always lightly explained. Although thus diversified in social beliefs, the residents became solidly united through our mutual experience in an industrial quarter, and we became not only convinced of the need for social control and protective legislation but also of the value of this preliminary argument. . . .

Chapter Ten

Pioneer Labor Legislation in Illinois

O UR VERY FIRST Christmas at Hull House, when we as yet knew nothing of child labor, a number of little girls refused the candy which was offered them as part of the Christmas good cheer, saying simply that they "worked in a candy factory and could not bear the sight of it." We discovered that for six weeks they had worked from seven in the morning until nine at night, and they were exhausted as well as satiated. The sharp consciousness of stern economic conditions was thus thrust upon us in the midst of the season of good will.

During the same winter three boys from a Hull House club were injured at one machine in a neighboring factory for lack of a guard which would have cost but a few dollars. When the injury of one of these boys resulted in his death, we felt quite sure that the owners of the factory would share our horror and remorse, and that they would do everything possible to prevent the recurrence of such a tragedy. To our surprise they did nothing whatever, and I made my first acquaintance then with those pathetic documents signed by the parents of working children, that they will make no claim for damages resulting from "carelessness."

The visits we made in the neighborhood constantly discovered women sewing upon sweatshop work, and often they were assisted by incredibly small children. I remember a little girl of four who pulled out basting threads hour after hour, sitting on a stool at the feet of her Bohemian mother, a little bunch of human misery. But even for that there was no legal redress, for the only child-labor law in Illinois, with any provision for enforcement, had been secured by the coal miners' unions, and was confined to children employed in mines.

We learned to know many families in which the working children contributed to the support of their parents, not only because they spoke English better than the older immigrants and were willing to take lower wages, but because their parents gradually found it easy to live upon their earnings. A South Italian peasant who has picked olives and packed oranges from his toddling babyhood cannot see at once the difference

between the outdoor healthy work which he had performed in the varying seasons, and the long hours of
monotonous factory life which his child encounters
when he goes to work in Chicago. An Italian father
came to us in great grief over the death of his eldest
child, a little girl of twelve, who had brought the largest
wages into the family fund. In the midst of his genuine
sorrow he said: "She was the oldest kid I had. Now I
shall have to go back to work again until the next one
is able to take care of me." The man was only thirty-
three and had hoped to retire from work at least during
the winters. . . . Another little girl of thirteen, a Russian-Jewish child employed in a laundry at a heavy task
beyond her strength, committed suicide, because she
had borrowed three dollars from a companion which
she could not repay unless she confided the story to her
parents and gave up an entire week's wages—but what
could the family live upon that week in case she did!
Her child mind, of course, had no sense of proportion,
and carbolic acid appeared inevitable.

While we found many pathetic cases of child labor
and hard-driven victims of the sweating system who
could not possibly earn enough in the short busy
season to support themselves during the rest of the
year, it became evident that we must add carefully
collected information to our general impression of
neighborhood conditions if we would make it of any
genuine value.

There was at that time no statistical information on Chicago industrial conditions, and Mrs. Florence Kelley, an early resident of Hull House, suggested to the Illinois State Bureau of Labor that they investigate the sweating system in Chicago with its attendant child labor. The head of the Bureau adopted this suggestion and engaged Mrs. Kelley to make the investigation. When the report was presented to the Illinois Legislature, a special committee was appointed to look into the Chicago conditions. I well recall that on the Sunday the members of this commission came to dine at Hull House, our hopes ran high, and we believed that at last some of the worst ills under which our neighbors were suffering would be brought to an end.

As a result of its investigations, this committee recommended to the Legislature the provisions which afterward became those of the first factory law of Illinois, regulating the sanitary conditions of the sweatshop and fixing fourteen as the age at which a child might be employed. Before the passage of the law could be secured, it was necessary to appeal to all elements of the community, and a little group of us addressed the open meetings of trades unions and of benefit societies, church organizations, and social clubs literally every evening for three months. Of course the most energetic help as well as intelligent understanding came from the trades unions. The central labor body of Chicago, then called the Trades and Labor Assembly, had previously appointed a committee of investigation to inquire into the sweating system. This committee consisted of five delegates from the unions and five outside their membership. Two of the latter were residents of Hull House, and continued with the tunions in their well-conducted campaign until the passage of Illinois's first Factory Legislation was secured, a statute which has gradually been built upon by many public-spirited citizens until Illinois stands well among the States, at least in the matter of protecting her children. The Hull House residents that winter had their first experience in lobbying. I remember that I very much disliked the word and still more the prospect of the lobbying itself, and we insisted that well-known Chicago women should accompany this first little group of Settlement folk who with trades unionists moved upon the state capitol in behalf of factory legislation. The national or, to use its formal name, The General Federation of Woman's Clubs, had been organized in Chicago only the year before this legislation was secured. The Federation was then timid in regard to all legislation because it was anxious not to frighten its new membership, although its second president, Mrs. Henrotin, was most untiring in her efforts to secure this law.

It was, perhaps, a premature effort, though certainly founded upon a genuine need, to urge that a clause limiting the hours of all women working in factories or workshops to eight a day, or forty-eight a week, should be inserted in the first factory legislation of the State. . . . One of our . . . most painful impressions of those first years is that of pale, listless girls, who worked regularly in a factory of the vicinity which was then running full night time. These girls also encountered a special danger in the early morning hours as they returned from work, debilitated and exhausted, and only too easily convinced that a drink and a little dancing at the end of the balls in the saloon dance halls, was what they needed to brace them. One of the girls whom we then knew, whose name, Chloe, seemed to fit her delicate charm, craving a drink to dispel her lassitude before her tired feet should take the long walk home, had thus been decoyed into a saloon, where the soft drink was followed by an alcoholic one containing "knockout drops," and she awoke in a disreputable rooming house—too frightened and disgraced to return to her mother.

… The eight-hour clause in this first factory law met with much less opposition in the Legislature than was anticipated, and was enforced for a year before it was pronounced unconstitutional by the Supreme Court of Illinois. . . .

This first attempt in Illinois for adequate factory legislation also was associated in the minds of businessmen with radicalism, because the law was secured during the term of Governor Altgeld and was first enforced during his administration. While nothing in its genesis or spirit could be further from "anarchy" than factory legislation, and while the first law in Illinois was still far behind Massachusetts and New York, the fact that Governor Altgeld pardoned from the state's prison the anarchists who had been sentenced there after the Haymarket riot, gave the opponents of this most reasonable legislation a quickly utilized opportunity. . . . The inception of the law had already become associated with Hull House, and when its ministration was also centered there, we inevitably received all the odium which these first efforts entailed. Mrs. Kelley was appointed the first factory inspector with a deputy and a force of twelve inspectors to enforce the law. Both Mrs. Kelley and her assistant, Mrs. Stevens, lived at Hull House; the office was on Polk Street directly opposite, and one of the most vigorous deputies was the president of the Jane Club. In addition, one of the early men residents, since dean of a state law school, acted as prosecutor in the cases brought against the violators of the law. . . .

During the fourth year of our residence at Hull House we found ourselves in a large mass meeting ardently advocating the passage of a Federal measure called the Sulzer Bill. Even in our short struggle with the evils of the sweating system it did not seem strange that the center of the effort had shifted to Washington, for by that time we had realized that the sanitary regulation of sweatshops by city officials, and a careful enforcement of factory legislation by state factory inspectors will not avail, unless each city and State shall be able to pass and enforce a code of comparatively uniform legislation. Although the Sulzer Act failed to utilize the Interstate Commerce legislation for its purpose, many of the national representatives realized for the first time that only by federal legislation could their constituents in remote country places be protected from contagious diseases raging in New York or Chicago, for many country doctors testify as to the outbreak of scarlet fever in rural neighborhoods after the children have begun to wear the winter overcoats and cloaks which have been sent from infected city sweatshops.

Through our efforts to modify the sweating system, the Hull House residents gradually became committed to the fortunes of the Consumers' League, an organization which for years has been approaching the question of the underpaid sewing woman from the point of view of the ultimate responsibility lodged in the consumer. It becomes more reasonable to make the presentation of the sweatshop situation through this League, as it is more effectual to work with them for the extension of legal provisions in the slow upbuilding of that code of legislation which is alone sufficient to protect the home from the dangers incident to the sweating system.

The Consumers' League seems to afford the best method of approach for the protection of girls in department stores; I recall a group of girls from a neighboring "emporium" who applied to Hull House for dancing parties on alternate Sunday afternoons. In reply to our protest they told us they not only worked late every evening, in spite of the fact that each was supposed to have "two nights a week off," and every Sunday morning, but that on alternate Sunday afternoons they were required "to sort the stock." Over and over again, meetings called by the Clerks Union and others have been held at Hull House protesting against these incredibly long hours. Little modification has come about, however, during our twenty years of residence, although one large store in the Bohemian quarter closes all day on Sunday and many of the others for three nights a week. . . .

The women shirt makers and the women cloak makers were both organized at Hull House as was also the Dorcas Federal Labor Union, which had been founded through the efforts of a working woman, then one of the residents. The latter union met once a month in our drawing room. It was composed of representatives from all the unions in the city which included women in their membership and also received other women in sympathy with unionism. It was accorded representation in the central labor body of the city, and later it joined its efforts with those of others to found the Woman's Union Label League. . . .

The Pullman strike afforded much illumination to many Chicago people. Before it, there had been nothing in my experience to reveal that distinct cleavage of society, which a general strike at least momentarily affords. Certainly, during all those dark days of the Pullman strike, the growth of class bitterness was most obvious. The fact that the Settlement maintained avenues of intercourse with both sides seemed to give it opportunity for nothing but a realization of the bitterness and division along class lines. I had known Mr. Pullman and had seen his genuine pride and pleasure in the model town he had built with so much care; and I had an opportunity to talk to many of the Pullman employees during the strike when I was sent from a so-called "Citizens' Arbitration Committee" to their first meetings held in a hall in the neighboring village of Kensington, and when I was invited to the modest supper tables laid in the model houses. The employees then expected a speedy settlement and no one doubted but that all the grievances connected with the "straw bosses" would be quickly remedied and that the benevolence which had built the model town would not fail them. They were sure that the "straw bosses" had misrepresented the state of affairs, for this very first awakening to class-consciousness bore many traces of the servility on one side and the arrogance on the other which had so long prevailed in the model town.

The entire strike demonstrated how often the outcome of far-reaching industrial disturbances is dependent upon the personal will of the employer or the temperament of a strike leader. Those familiar with strikes know only too well how much they are influenced by poignant domestic situations, by the troubled consciences of the minority directors, by the suffering women and children, by the keen excitement of the struggle, by the religious scruples sternly suppressed but occasionally asserting themselves, now on one side and now on the other, and by that undefined psychology of the crowd which we understand so little. All of these factors also influence the public and do much to determine popular sympathy and judgment. In the early days of the Pullman strike, as I was coming down in the elevator of the Auditorium hotel from one of the futile meetings of the Arbitration Committee, I met an acquaintance, who angrily said "that the strikers ought all to be shot." As I had heard nothing so bloodthirsty as this either from the most enraged capitalist or from the most desperate of the men, and was interested to find the cause of such a senseless outbreak, I finally discovered that the first ten thousand dollars which my acquaintance had ever saved, requiring, he said, years of effort from the time he was twelve years old until he was thirty, had been lost as the result of a strike; he clinched his argument that he knew what he was talking about, with the statement that "no one need expect him to have any sympathy with strikers or with their affairs."

A very intimate and personal experience revealed, at least to myself, my constant dread of the spreading ill will. At the height of the sympathetic strike my oldest sister, who was convalescing from a long illness in a hospital near Chicago, became suddenly very much worse. While I was able to reach her at once, every possible obstacle of a delayed and blocked transportation system interrupted the journey of her husband and children who were hurrying to her bedside from a distant state. As the end drew nearer and I was obliged to reply to my sister's constant inquiries that her family had not yet come, I was filled with a profound apprehension lest her last hours should be touched with resentment toward those responsible for the delay; lest her unutterable longing should at the very end be tinged with bitterness. She must have divined what was in my mind, for at last she said each time after the repetition of my sad news: "I don't blame anyone, I am not judging them." My heart was comforted and heavy at the same time; but how many more such moments of sorrow and death were being made difficult and lonely throughout the land, and how much would these experiences add to the lasting bitterness, that touch of self-righteousness which makes the spirit of forgiveness well nigh impossible.

When I returned to Chicago from the quiet country I saw the Federal troops encamped about the post office; almost everyone on Halsted Street wearing a white ribbon, the emblem of the strikers' side; the residents at Hull House divided in opinion as to the righteousness of this or that measure; and no one able to secure any real information as to which side was burning the cars. After the Pullman strike I made an attempt to analyze in a paper which I called "The Modern King Lear" the inevitable revolt of human nature against the plans Mr. Pullman had made for his employees, the miscarriage of which appeared to him such black ingratitude. It seemed to me unendurable not to make some effort to gather together the social implications of the failure of this benevolent employer and its relation to the demand for a more democratic administration of industry. Doubtless the paper represented a certain "excess of participation," to use a gentle phrase of Charles Lamb's in preference to a more emphatic one used by Mr. Pullman himself. The last picture of the Pullman strike which I distinctly recall was three years later when one of the strike leaders came to see me. Although out of work for most of the time since the strike, he had been undisturbed for six months in the repair shops of a streetcar company, under an assumed name, but he had at that moment been discovered and dismissed. He was a superior type of English workingman, but as he stood there, broken and discouraged, believing himself so black-listed that his skill could never be used again, filled with sorrow over the loss of his wife who had recently died after an illness with distressing mental symptoms, realizing keenly the lack of the respectable way of living he had always until now been able to maintain, he seemed to me an epitome of the wretched human waste such a strike implies. I fervently hoped that the new arbitration law would prohibit in Chicago forever more such brutal and ineffective methods of settling industrial disputes. And yet even as early as 1896, we found the greatest difficulty in applying the arbitration law to the garment workers' strike, although it was finally accomplished after various mass meetings had urged it. . . .

But of all the aspects of social misery nothing is so heartbreaking as unemployment, and it was inevitable that we should see much of it in a neighborhood where low rents attracted the poorly paid worker and many newly arrived immigrants who were first employed in gangs upon railroad extensions and similar undertakings. The sturdy peasants eager for work were either the victims of the padrone who fleeced them unmercifully, both in securing a place to work and then in supplying them with food, or they became the mere sport of unscrupulous employment agencies. Hull House made an investigation both of the padrone and of the agencies in our immediate vicinity, and the outcome confirming what we already suspected, we eagerly threw ourselves into a movement to procure free employment bureaus under State control until a law authorizing such bureaus and giving the officials entrusted with their management power to regulate private employment agencies, passed the Illinois Legislature in 1899. The history of these bureaus demonstrates the tendency we all have to consider a legal enactment in itself an achievement and to grow careless in regard to its administration and actual results; for an investigation into the situation ten years later discovered that immigrants were still shamefully imposed upon. A group of Bulgarians were found who had been sent to work in Arkansas where their services were not needed; they walked back to Chicago only to secure their next job in Oklahoma and to pay another railroad fare as well as another commission to the agency. . . .

This investigation of the employment bureau resources of Chicago was undertaken by the League for the Protection of Immigrants, with whom it is possible for Hull House to cooperate whenever an investigation of the immigrant colonies in our immediate neighborhood seems necessary, as was recently done in regard to the Greek colonies of Chicago. The superintendent of this League, Miss Grace Abbott, is a resident of Hull House and all of our later attempts to secure justice and opportunity for immigrants are much more effective through the League, and when we speak before a congressional committee in Washington concerning the needs of Chicago immigrants, we represent the League as well as our own neighbors. . . .

The stormy teamsters' strike, ostensibly undertaken in defense of the garment workers, but really arising from causes so obscure and dishonorable that they have never yet been made public, was the culmination of a type of trades unions which had developed in Chicago during the preceding decade in which corruption had flourished almost as openly as it had previously done in the City Hall. This corruption sometimes took the form of grafting after the manner of Samuel Parks in New York; sometimes that of political deals in the "delivery of the labor vote"; and sometimes that of a combination between capital and labor hunting together. At various times during these years the better type of trades unionists had made a firm stand against this corruption and a determined effort to eradicate it from the labor movement, not unlike the general reform effort of many American cities against political corruption. This reform movement in the Chicago Federation of Labor had its martyrs, and more than one man nearly lost his life through the "slugging" methods employed by the powerful corruptionists. And yet even in the midst of these things were found touching examples of fidelity to the earlier principles of brotherhood totally untouched by the corruption. At one time the scrubwomen in the downtown office buildings had a union of their own affiliated with the elevator men and the janitors. Although the union was used merely as a weapon in the fight of the coal teamsters against the use of natural gas in downtown buildings, it did not prevent the women from getting their first glimpse into the fellowship and the sense of protection which is the great gift of trades unionism to the unskilled, unbefriended worker. I remember in a meeting held at Hull House one Sunday afternoon, that the president of a "local" of scrubwomen stood up to relate her experience. She told first of the long years in which the fear of losing her job and the fluctuating pay were harder to bear than the hard work itself, when she had regarded all the other women who scrubbed in the same building merely as rivals and was most afraid of the most miserable, because they offered to work for less and less as they were pressed harder and harder by debt. Then she told of the change that had come when the elevator men and even the lordly janitors had talked to her about an organization and had said that they must all stand together. She told how gradually she came to feel sure of her job and of her regular pay, and she was even starting to buy a house now that she could "calculate" how much she "could have for sure." Neither she nor any of the other members

knew that the same combination which had organized the scrubwomen into a union later destroyed it
during a strike inaugurated for their own purposes.

That a Settlement is drawn into the labor issues of
its city can seem remote to its purpose only to those
who fail to realize that so far as the present industrial system thwarts our ethical demands, not only for
social righteousness but for social order, a Settlement
is committed to an effort to understand and, as far as
possible, to alleviate it. That in this effort it should be
drawn into fellowship with the local efforts of trades
unions is most obvious. This identity of aim apparently commits the Settlement in the public mind to
all the faiths and works of actual trades unions. . . .

. . . The reaction of strikes upon Chicago Settlements
affords an interesting study in social psychology. For
whether Hull House is in any wise identified with the
strike or not, makes no difference. When "Labor" is
in disgrace we are always regarded as belonging to it
and share the opprobrium. In the public excitement
following the Pullman strike, Hull House lost many
friends; later the teamsters' strike caused another such
defection, although my office in both cases had been
solely that of a duly appointed arbitrator. . . .

There has gradually developed between the various
Settlements of Chicago a warm fellowship founded
upon a like-mindedness resulting from similar experiences, quite as identity of interest and endeavor

develop an enduring relation between the residents of the same Settlement. This sense of comradeship is never stronger than during the hardships and perplexities of a strike of unskilled workers revolting against the conditions which drag them even below the level of their European life. At such time the residents in various Settlements are driven to a standard of life argument running somewhat in this wise—that as the very existence of the State depends upon the character of its citizens, therefore if certain industrial conditions are forcing the workers below the standard of decency, it becomes possible to deduce the right of State regulation. Even as late as the stockyard strike this line of argument was denounced as "socialism" although it has since been confirmed as wise statesmanship by a decision of the Supreme Court of the United States which was apparently secured through the masterly argument of the Brandeis brief in the Oregon ten-hour case.

In such wise the residents of an industrial neighborhood gradually comprehend the close connection of their own difficulties with national and even international movements. The residents in the Chicago Settlements became pioneer members in the American branch of the International League for Labor Legislation, because their neighborhood experiences had made them only too conscious of the dire need for protective legislation. . . .

Chapter Eleven

Immigrants and Their Children

FOR SEVERAL YEARS, every Saturday evening the entire families of our Italian neighbors were our guests. These evenings were very popular during our first winters at Hull House. Many educated Italians helped us, and the house became known as a place where Italians were welcome and where national holidays were observed. They come to us with their petty lawsuits, sad relics of the *vendetta*, with their incorrigible boys, with their hospital cases, with their aspirations for American clothes, and with their needs for an interpreter.

An editor of an Italian paper made a genuine connection between us and the Italian colony, not only with the Neapolitans and the Sicilians of the imme-diate neighborhood, but with the educated *connazi-onali* throughout the city, until he went south to start an agricultural colony in Alabama, in the establish-ment of which Hull House heartily cooperated.

Possibly the South Italians more than any other immigrants represent the pathetic stupidity of agri-cultural people crowded into city tenements, and we were much gratified when thirty peasant fami-lies were induced to move upon the land which they knew so well how to cultivate. The starting of this col-ony, however, was a very expensive affair in spite of the fact that the colonists purchased the land at two dollars an acre; they needed much more than raw land, and although it was possible to collect the small sums necessary to sustain them during the hard time of the first two years, we were fully convinced that undertakings of this sort could be conducted prop-erly only by colonization societies such as England has established, or, better still, by enlarging the func-tions of the Federal Department of Immigration.

An evening similar in purpose to the one devoted to the Italians was organized for the Germans, in our first year. Owing to the superior education of our Teutonic guests and the clever leading of a cultivated German woman, these evenings reflected something of that cozy social intercourse which is found in its perfection in the fatherland. Our guests sang a great deal in the tender minor of the German folksong or in the rousing spirit of the Rhine, and they slowly but persistently pursued a course in German history and literature, recovering something of that poetry and romance which they had long since resigned with other good things. . . .

An overmastering desire to reveal the humbler immigrant parents to their own children lay at the base of what has come to be called the Hull House Labor Museum. . . .

We found in the immediate neighborhood at least four varieties of the . . . most primitive methods of spinning and three distinct variations of the same spindle in connection with wheels. It was possible to put these seven into historic sequence and order and to connect the whole with the present method of factory spinning. The same thing was done for weaving, and on every Saturday evening a little exhibit was made of these various forms of labor in the textile industry. . . .

. . . The textile museum is connected directly with the basket weaving, sewing, millinery, embroidery, and dressmaking constantly being taught at Hull House, and so far as possible with the other educational departments; we have also been able to make a collection of products, of early implements, and of photographs which are full of suggestion. . . .

In some such ways as these have the Labor Museum and the shops pointed out the possibilities which Hull

House has scarcely begun to develop, of demonstrating that culture is an understanding of the long-established occupations and thoughts of men, of the arts with which they have solaced their toil. A yearning to recover for the household arts something of their early sanctity and meaning arose strongly within me one evening when I was attending a Passover Feast to which I had been invited by a Jewish family in the neighborhood, where the traditional and religious significance of the woman's daily activity was still retained. The kosher food the Jewish mother spread before her family had been prepared according to traditional knowledge and with constant care in the use of utensils; upon her had fallen the responsibility to make all ready according to Mosaic instructions that the great crisis in a religious history might be fittingly set forth by her husband and son. . . .

There are many examples of touching fidelity to immigrant customs and parents on the part of their grown children; a young man who day after day attends ceremonies which no longer express his religious convictions and who makes his vain effort to interest his Russian Jewish father in social problems; a daughter who might earn much more money as a stenographer could she work from Monday morning till Saturday night, but who quietly and docilely makes neckties for low wages because she can thus abstain from work Saturdays to please her father. . . .

This faithfulness, however, is sometimes ruthlessly imposed upon by immigrant parents who, eager for money and accustomed to the patriarchal authority of peasant households, hold their children in a stern bondage which requires a surrender of all their wages and concedes no time or money for pleasures.

There are many convincing illustrations that this parental harshness often results in juvenile delinquency. A Polish boy of seventeen came to Hull House one day to ask a contribution of fifty cents "towards a flower piece for the funeral of an old Hull House club boy." A few questions made it clear that the object was fictitious, whereupon the boy broke down and half-defiantly stated that he wanted to buy two twenty-five cent tickets, one for his girl and one for himself, to a dance of the Benevolent Social Twos; that he hadn't a penny of his own although he had worked in a brass foundry for three years and had been advanced twice, because he always had to give his pay envelope unopened to his father; "just look at the clothes he buys me" was his concluding remark.

Perhaps the girls are held even more rigidly. In a recent investigation of two hundred working girls it was found that only five per cent had the use of their own money and that sixty-two per cent turned in all they earned, literally every penny, to their mothers. It was through this little investigation that we first knew Marcella, a pretty young German girl who helped her widowed mother year after year to care for a large family of younger children. She was content for the most part although her mother's old-country notions of dress gave her but an infinitesimal amount of her own wages to spend on her clothes, and she was quite sophisticated as to proper dressing because she sold silk in a neighborhood department store. Her mother approved of the young man who was showing her various attentions and agreed that Marcella should accept his invitation to a ball, but would allow her not a penny toward a new gown to replace one impossibly plain and shabby. Marcella spent a sleepless night and wept bitterly, although she well knew that the doctor's bill for the children's scarlet fever was not yet paid. The next day as she was cutting off three yards of shining pink silk, the thought came to her that it would make her a fine new waist to wear to the ball. She wistfully saw it wrapped in paper and carelessly stuffed into the muff of the purchaser, when suddenly the parcel fell upon the floor. No one was looking and quick as a flash the girl picked it up and pushed it into her blouse. The theft was discovered by the relentless department store detective who, for "the sake of example," insisted upon taking the case into court. The poor mother wept bitter tears over this downfall of her "*frommes Mädchen*" and no one had the heart to tell her of her own blindness.

I know a Polish boy whose earnings were all given to his father who gruffly refused all requests for pocket money. One Christmas his little sisters, having been told by their mother that they were too poor to have any Christmas presents, appealed to the big brother as to one who was earning money of his own. Flattered by the implication, but at the same time quite impecunious, the night before Christmas he nonchalantly walked through a neighboring department store and stole a manicure set for one little sister and a string of beads for the other. He was caught at the door by the house detective as one of those children whom each local department store arrests in the weeks before Christmas at the daily rate of eight to twenty. . . .

Many of these children have come to grief through their premature fling into city life, having thrown off parental control as they have impatiently discarded foreign ways. Boys of ten and twelve will refuse to sleep at home, preferring the freedom of an old brewery vault or an empty warehouse to the obedience required by their parents, and for days these boys will live on the milk and bread which they steal from the back porches after the early morning delivery. Such children complain that there is "no fun" at home. One little chap who was given a vacant lot to cultivate by the City Garden Association insisted upon raising only popcorn and tried to present the entire crop to Hull House "to be used for the parties," with the stipulation that he would have "to be invited every single time. . . ."

It is difficult to write of the relation of the older and most foreign-looking immigrants to the children of other people—the Italians whose fruit carts are upset simply because they are "dagoes," or the Russian peddlers who are stoned and sometimes badly injured because it has become a code of honor in a gang of boys to thus express their derision. The members of a Protective Association of Jewish Peddlers organized at Hull House related daily experiences in which old age had been treated with . . . irreverence, cherished dignity with . . . disrespect. . . . The Greeks are filled with amazed rage when their very name is flung at them as an opprobrious epithet. Doubtless these difficulties would be much minimized in America, if we faced our own race problem with courage and intelligence, and these very Mediterranean immigrants might give us valuable help. Certainly they are less conscious than the Anglo-Saxon of color distinctions, perhaps because of their traditional familiarity with Carthage and Egypt. They listened with respect and enthusiasm to a scholarly address delivered by Professor Du Bois at Hull House on a Lincoln's birthday, with apparently no consciousness of that race difference which color seems to accentuate so absurdly, and upon my return from various conferences held in the interest of "the advancement of colored people," I have had many illuminating conversations with my cosmopolitan neighbors. . . .

A huge Hellenic meeting held at Hull House, in which the achievements of the classic period were set forth both in Greek and English by scholars of well-known repute, brought us into a new sense of fellowship with all our Greek neighbors. As the mayor of Chicago was seated upon the right hand of the dignified senior priest of the Greek Church and they were greeted alternately in the national hymns of America and Greece, one felt a curious sense of the possibility of transplanting to new and crude Chicago some of the traditions of Athens itself, so deeply cherished in the hearts of this group of citizens. . . .

To me personally the celebration of the hundredth anniversary of Mazzini's birth was a matter of great interest. Throughout the world that day Italians who believed in a United Italy came together. They recalled the hopes of this man who, with all his devotion to his country was still more devoted to humanity and who dedicated to the workingmen of Italy, an appeal so philosophical, so filled with a yearning for righteousness, that it transcended all national boundaries and became a bugle call for "The Duties of Man." A copy of this document was given to every school child in the public schools of Italy on this one hundredth anniversary, and . . . the Chicago branch of the Society of Young Italy marched into our largest hall and presented to Hull House an heroic bust of Mazzini. . . .

Chapter Twelve

Tolstoyism

THE ADMINISTRATION OF charity in Chicago during the winter following the World's Fair had been of necessity most difficult, for, although large sums had been given to the temporary relief organization which endeavored to care for the thousands of destitute strangers stranded in the city, we all worked under a sense of desperate need and a paralyzing consciousness that our best efforts were most inadequate to the situation.

During the many relief visits I paid that winter in tenement houses and miserable lodgings, I was constantly shadowed by a certain sense of shame that I should be comfortable in the midst of such distress. This resulted at times in a curious reaction against all the educational and philanthropic activities in which I had been engaged. In the face of the desperate hunger and need, these could not but seem futile and superficial. . . .

. . . Dealing directly with the simplest human wants may have been responsible for an impression which I carried about with me almost constantly for a period of two years and which culminated finally in a visit to Tolstoy—that the Settlement, or Hull House at least, was a mere pretense and travesty of the simple impulse "to live with the poor," so long as the residents did not share the common lot of hard labor and scant fare.

Actual experience had left me in much the same state of mind I had been in after reading Tolstoy's *What to Do*, which is a description of his futile efforts to relieve the unspeakable distress and want in the Moscow winter of 1881, and his inevitable conviction that only he who literally shares his own shelter and food with the needy can claim to have served them. . . .

I had read the books of Tolstoy steadily all the years since *My Religion* had come into my hands immediately after I left college. . . . But I was most eager to know whether Tolstoy's undertaking to do his daily share of the physical labor of the world had brought him peace. . . .

I had time to review carefully many things in my mind during the long days of convalescence following an illness of typhoid fever which I suffered in the autumn of 1895. The illness was so prolonged that my health was most unsatisfactory during the following winter, and the next May I went abroad with my friend, Miss Smith, to effect if possible a more complete recovery.

The prospect of seeing Tolstoy filled me with the hope of finding a clue to the tangled affairs of city poverty. I was but one of thousands of our contemporaries who were turning toward this Russian, not as to a seer—his message is much too confused and contradictory for that—but as to a man who has had the ability to lift his life to the level of his conscience, to translate his theories into action.

Our first few weeks in England were most stimulating. A dozen years ago London still showed traces of "that exciting moment in the life of the nation when its youth is casting about for new enthusiasms," but it evinced still more of that British capacity to perform the hard work of careful research and self-examination which must precede any successful experiments in social reform. . . .

We heard Keir Hardie before a large audience of workingmen standing in the open square of Canning Town outline the great things to be accomplished by the then new Labor Party, and we joined the vast body of men in the booming hymn "When wilt Thou save the people, / O God of Mercy, when!" finding it hard to realize that we were attending a political meeting. It seemed that moment as if the hopes of democracy were more likely to come to pass on English soil than upon our own. . . .

While all this was warmly human, we also had opportunities to see something of a group of men and women who were approaching the social problem from the study of economics; among others Mr. and Mrs. Sidney Webb who were at work on their Industrial Democracy; Mr. John Hobson who was lecturing on the evolution of modern capitalism.

We followed factory inspectors on a round of duties performed with a thoroughness and a trained intelligence which were a revelation of the possibilities of public service. . . .

One evening in University Hall Mrs. Humphry Ward, who had just returned from Italy, described the effect of the Italian salt tax in a talk which was evidently one in a series of lectures upon the economic wrongs which pressed heaviest upon the poor. . . . The entire impression received in England of research, of scholarship, of organized public spirit, was in marked contrast to the impressions of my next visit in 1900, when the South African War had absorbed the enthusiasm of the nation and the wrongs at "the heart of the empire" were disregarded and neglected.

London, of course, presented sharp differences to Russia where social conditions were written in black and white with little shading, like a demonstration of the Chinese proverb, "Where one man lives in luxury, another is dying of hunger. . . ."

We had letters of introduction to Mr. and Mrs. Aylmer Maude of Moscow, since well known as the translators of *Resurrection* and other of Tolstoy's later works, who at that moment were on the eve of leaving Russia in order to form an agricultural colony in South England where they might support themselves by the labor of their hands. We gladly accepted Mr. Maude's offer to take us to Yasnaya Polyana and to introduce us to Count Tolstoy, and never did a disciple journey toward his master with more enthusiasm than did our guide. When, however, Mr. Maude actually presented Miss Smith and myself to Count Tolstoy, knowing well his master's attitude toward philanthropy, he endeavored to make Hull House appear much more noble and unique than I should have ventured to do.

Tolstoy, standing by clad in his peasant garb, listened gravely but, glancing distrustfully at the sleeves of my traveling gown which unfortunately at that season were monstrous in size, he took hold of an edge and pulling out one sleeve to an interminable breadth, said quite simply that "there was enough stuff on one arm to make a frock for a little girl," and asked me directly if I did not find "such a dress" a "barrier to the people." I was too disconcerted to make a very clear explanation. . . . Fortunately the countess came to my rescue with a recital of her former attempts to clothe hypothetical little girls in yards of material cut from a train and other superfluous parts of her best gown until she had been driven to a firm stand which she advised me to take at once. But neither Countess Tolstoy nor any other friend was on hand to help me out of my predicament later, when I was asked who "fed" me, and how did I obtain "shelter"? Upon my reply that a farm a hundred miles from Chicago supplied me with the necessities of life, I fairly anticipated the next scathing question: "So you are an absentee landlord? Do you think you will help the people more by adding yourself to the crowded city than you would by tilling your own soil?" This new sense of discomfort over a failure to till my own soil was increased when Tolstoy's second daughter appeared at the five o'clock tea table set under the trees, coming straight from the harvest field where she had been working with a group of peasants since five o'clock in the morning, not pretending to work but really taking the place of a peasant woman who had hurt her foot. She was plainly much exhausted, but neither expected nor received sympathy from the members of a family who were quite accustomed to see each other carry out their convictions in spite of discomfort and fatigue. . . .

That summer evening as we sat in the garden with a group of visitors from Germany, from England and

America, who had traveled to the remote Russian village that they might learn of this man, one could not forbear the constant inquiry to one's self, as to why he was so regarded as sage and saint that this party of people should be repeated each day of the year. It seemed to me then that we were all attracted by this sermon of the deed, because Tolstoy had made the one supreme personal effort, one might almost say the one frantic personal effort, to put himself into right relations with the humblest people, with the men who tilled his soil, blacked his boots, and cleaned his stables. Doubtless the heaviest burden of our contemporaries is a consciousness of a divergence between our democratic theory on the one hand, that working people have a right to the intellectual resources of society, and the actual fact on the other hand, that thousands of them are so overburdened with toil that there is no leisure nor energy left for the cultivation of the mind. We constantly suffer from the strain and indecision of believing this theory and acting as if we did not believe it, and this man who years before had tried "to get off the backs of the peasants," who had at least simplified his life and worked with his hands, had come to be a prototype to many of his generation. . . .

At the long dinner table laid in the garden were the various traveling guests, the grown-up daughters, and the younger children with their governess. The countess presided over the usual European dinner served by men, but the count and the daughter, who had worked all day in the fields, ate only porridge and black bread and drank only kvas, the fare of the hay-making peasants. Of course we are all accustomed to the fact that those who perform the heaviest labor eat the coarsest and simplest fare at the end of the day, but it is not often that we sit at the same table with them while we ourselves eat the more elaborate food prepared by someone else's labor. Tolstoy ate his simple supper without remark or comment upon the food his family and guests preferred to eat, assuming that they, as well as he, had settled the matter with their own consciences. . . .

The conversation at dinner and afterward, although conducted with animation and sincerity, for the moment stirred vague misgivings within me. Was Tolstoy more logical than life warrants? Could the wrongs of life be reduced to the terms of unre-quited labor and all be made right if each person performed the amount necessary to satisfy his own wants? . . . A horde of perplexing questions, concerning those problems of existence of which in happier moments we catch but fleeting glimpses and at which we even then stand aghast, pursued us relentlessly on the long journey through the great wheat plains of South Russia, through the crowded Ghetto of War-saw, and finally into the smiling fields of Germany where the peasant men and women were harvesting the grain. . . .

. . . During the next month in Germany, when I read everything of Tolstoy's that had been translated into English, German, or French, there grew up in my mind a conviction that what I ought to do upon my return to Hull House was to spend at least two hours every morning in the little bakery which we had recently added to the equipment of our coffeehouse. Two hours' work would be but a wretched compromise, but it was hard to see how I could take more time out of each day. I had been taught to bake bread in my childhood not only as a household accomplishment, but because my father, true to his miller's tradition, had insisted that each one of his daughters on her twelfth birthday must present him with a satisfactory wheat loaf of her own baking, and he was most exigent as to the quality of this test loaf. What could be more in keeping with my training and tradition than baking bread? I did not quite see how my activity would fit in with that of the German union baker who presided over the Hull House bakery, but all such matters were secondary and certainly could be arranged. It may be that I had thus to pacify my aroused conscience before I could settle down to hear Wagner's "Ring" at Beyreuth; it may be that I had fallen a victim to the phrase, "bread labor"; but at any rate I held fast to the belief that I should do this, through the entire journey homeward, on land and sea, until I actually arrived in Chicago when suddenly the whole scheme seemed to me as utterly preposterous as it doubtless was. The half dozen people invariably waiting to see me after breakfast, the piles of letters to be opened and answered, the demand of actual and pressing wants—were these all to be pushed aside and asked to wait while I saved my soul by two hours' work at baking bread?

Although my resolution was abandoned, this may be the best place to record the efforts of more doughty souls to carry out Tolstoy's conclusions. It was perhaps inevitable that Tolstoy colonies should be founded, although Tolstoy himself has always insisted that each man should live his life as nearly as possible in the place in which he was born. The visit Miss Smith and I made a year or two later to a colony in one of the southern States portrayed for us most vividly both the weakness and the strange august dignity of the Tolstoy position. The colonists at Commonwealth held but a short creed. They claimed in fact that the difficulty is not to state truth but to make moral conviction operative upon actual life, and they announced it their intention "to obey the teachings of Jesus in all matters of labor and the use of property." They would thus transfer the vindication of creed from the church to the open field, from dogma to experience.

The day Miss Smith and I visited the Commonwealth colony of threescore souls, they were erecting a house for the family of a one-legged man, consisting of a wife and nine children who had come the week before in a forlorn prairie schooner from Arkansas. As this was the largest family the little colony contained, the new house was to be the largest yet erected. Upon our surprise at this literal giving "to him that asketh," we inquired if the policy of extending food and shelter to all who applied, without test of creed or ability, might not result in the migration of all the neighboring poorhouse population into the colony. We were told that this actually had happened during the winter until the colony fare of corn meal and cow peas had proved so unattractive that the paupers had gone back, for even the poorest of the southern poorhouses occasionally supplied bacon with the pone if only to prevent scurvy from which the colonists themselves had suffered. The difficulty of the poorhouse people had thus settled itself by the sheer poverty of the situation, a poverty so biting that the only ones willing to face it were those sustained by a conviction of its righteousness. The fields and gardens were being worked by an editor, a professor, a clergyman, as well as by artisans and laborers, the fruit thereof to be eaten by themselves and their families or by any other families who might arrive from Arkansas. The colonists were very conventional in matters of family relationship and had broken with society only in regard to the conventions pertaining to labor and property. . . .

I knew little about the colony started by Mr. Maude at Purleigh containing several of Tolstoy's followers who were not permitted to live in Russia, and we did not see Mr. Maude again until he came to Chicago on his way from Manitoba, whither he had transported the second group of Dukhobors, a religious sect who had interested all of Tolstoy's followers because of their literal acceptance of nonresistance and other Christian doctrines which are so strenuously advocated by Tolstoy. It was for their benefit that Tolstoy had finished and published *Resurrection*, breaking through his long-kept resolution against novel writing. After the Dukhobors were settled in Canada, of the five hundred dollars left from the *Resurrection* funds, one-half was given to Hull House. It seemed possible to spend this fund only for the relief of the most primitive wants of food and shelter on the part of the most-needy families.

Chapter Thirteen

Public Activities and Investigations

IT IS EASY for even the most conscientious citizen of Chicago to forget the foul smells of the stockyards and the garbage dumps, when he is living so far from them that he is only occasionally made conscious of their existence, but the residents of a Settlement are perforce constantly surrounded by them. During our first three years on Halsted Street, we had established a small incinerator at Hull House and we had many times reported the untoward conditions of the ward to the city hall. We had also arranged many talks for the immigrants, pointing out that although a woman may sweep her own doorway in her native village and allow the refuse to innocently decay in the open air and sunshine, in a crowded city quarter, if the garbage is not properly collected and destroyed, a tenement house mother may see her children sicken and die, and that the immigrants must therefore not only keep their own houses clean, but must also help the authorities to keep the city clean.

Possibly our efforts slightly modified the worst conditions, but they still remained intolerable, and the fourth summer the situation became for me absolutely desperate when I realized in a moment of panic that my delicate little nephew for whom I was guardian, could not be with me at Hull House at all unless the sickening odors were reduced. I may well be ashamed that other delicate children who were torn from their families, not into boarding school but into eternity, had not long before driven me to effective action. Under the direction of the first man who came as a resident to Hull House we began a systematic investigation of the city system of garbage collection, both as to its efficiency in other wards and its possible connection with the death rate in the various wards of the city.

The Hull House Woman's Club had been organized the year before by the resident kindergartner who had first inaugurated a mother's meeting. The new members came together, however, in quite a new way that summer when we discussed with them the high death rate so persistent in our ward. After several club meetings devoted to the subject, despite the fact that the death rate rose highest in the congested foreign colonies and not in the streets in which most of the Irish American club women lived, twelve of their number undertook in connection with the residents, to carefully investigate the conditions of the alleys. During August and September the substantiated reports of violations of the law sent in from Hull House to the health department were one thousand and thirty-seven. For the club woman who had finished a long day's work of washing or ironing followed by the cooking of a hot supper, it would have been much easier to sit on her doorstep during a summer evening than to go up and down ill-kept alleys and get into trouble with her neighbors over the condition of their garbage boxes. It required both civic enterprise and moral conviction to be willing to do this three evenings a week during the hottest and most uncomfortable months of the year. Nevertheless, a certain number of women persisted, as did the residents, and three city inspectors in succession were transferred from the ward because of unsatisfactory services. Still the death rate remained high and the condition seemed little improved throughout the next winter. In sheer desperation, the following spring when the city contracts were awarded for the removal of garbage, with the backing of two well-known businessmen, I put in a bid for the garbage removal of the nineteenth ward. My paper was thrown out on a technicality but the incident induced the mayor to appoint me the garbage inspector of the ward.

The salary was a thousand dollars a year, and the loss of that political "plum" made a great stir among the politicians. The position was no sinecure whether regarded from the point of view of getting up at six in the morning to see that the men were early at work; or of following the loaded wagons, uneasily dropping their contents at intervals, to their dreary destination at the dump; or of insisting that the contractor must increase the number of his wagons from nine to thirteen and from thirteen to seventeen, although he assured me that he lost money on every one and that the former inspector had let him off with seven; or of taking careless landlords into court because they would not provide the proper garbage receptacles; or of arresting the tenant who tried to make the garbage wagons carry away the contents of his stable.

With the two or three residents who nobly stood by, we set up six of those doleful incinerators which are supposed to burn garbage with the fuel collected in the alley itself. The one factory in town which could utilize old tin cans was a window weight factory, and we deluged that with ten times as many tin cans as it could use—much less would pay for. We made desperate attempts to have the dead animals removed by the contractor who was paid most liberally by the city for that purpose but who, we slowly discovered, always made the police ambulances do the work, delivering the carcasses upon freight cars for shipment to a soap factory in Indiana where they were sold for a good price although the contractor himself was the largest stockholder in the concern. Perhaps our greatest achievement was the discovery of a pavement eighteen inches under the surface in a narrow street, although after it was found we triumphantly discovered a record of its existence in the city archives. The Italians living on the street were much interested but displayed little astonishment, perhaps because they were accustomed to see buried cities exhumed. This pavement became the *casus belli* between myself and the street commissioner when I insisted that its restoration belonged to him, after I had removed the first eight inches of garbage. The matter was finally settled by the mayor himself, who permitted me to drive him to the entrance of the street in what the children called my "garbage phaeton" and who took my side of the controversy.

A graduate of the University of Wisconsin, who had done some excellent volunteer inspection in both Chicago and Pittsburg, became my deputy and performed the work in a most thoroughgoing manner for three years. During the last two she was under the regime of civil service for in 1895, to the great joy of many citizens, the Illinois legislature made that possible. . . .

. . . Careful inspection combined with other causes, brought about a great improvement in the cleanliness and comfort of the neighborhood and one happy day, when the death rate of our ward was found to have dropped from third to seventh in the list of city wards and was so reported to our Woman's Club, the applause which followed recorded the genuine sense of participation in the result, and a public spirit which had "made good." But the cleanliness of the ward was becoming much too popular to suit our all-powerful alderman and, although we felt fatuously secure under the regime of civil service, he found a way to circumvent us by eliminating the position altogether. He introduced an ordinance into the city council which combined the collection of refuse with the cleaning and repairing of the streets, the whole to be placed under a ward superintendent. The office of course was to be filled under civil service regulations but only men were eligible to the examination. Although this latter regulation was afterwards modified in favor of one woman, it was retained long enough to put the nineteenth ward inspector out of office. . . .

. . . In the summer of 1902 during an epidemic of typhoid fever in which our ward, although containing but one thirty-sixth of the population of the city, registered one sixth of the total number of deaths, two of the Hull House residents made an investigation of the methods of plumbing in the houses adjacent to con-spicuous groups of fever cases. . . .

The careful information collected concerning the juxtaposition of the typhoid cases to the various systems of plumbing and nonplumbing was made the basis of a bacteriological study by another resident, Dr. Alice Hamilton, as to the possibility of the infection having been carried by flies. Her researches were so convincing that they have been incorporated into the body of scientific data supporting that theory, but there were also practical results from the investigation. It was discovered that the wretched sanitary appliances through which alone the infection could have become so widely spread, would not have been permitted to remain, unless the city inspector had either been criminally careless or open to the arguments of favored landlords.

The agitation finally resulted in a long and stirring trial before the civil service board of half of the employees in the Sanitary Bureau, with the final discharge of eleven out of the entire force of twenty-four. The inspector in our neighborhood was a kindly old man, greatly distressed over the affair, and quite unable to understand why he should have not used his discretion as to the time when a landlord should be forced to put in modern appliances. If he was "very poor," or "just about to sell his place," or "sure that the house would be torn down to make room for a factory," why should one "inconvenience" him? The old man died soon after the trial, feeling persecuted to the very last and not in the least understanding what it was all about. We were amazed at the commercial ramifications which graft in the city hall involved and at the indignation which interference with it produced. Hull House lost some large subscriptions as the result of this investigation, a loss which, if not easy to bear, was at least comprehensible. We also uncovered unexpected graft in connection with the plumbers' unions, and but for the fearless testimony of one of their members, could never have brought the trial to a successful issue.

Inevitable misunderstanding also developed in connection with the attempt on the part of Hull House residents to prohibit the sale of cocaine to minors, which brought us into sharp conflict with many druggists. I recall an Italian druggist living on the edge of the neighborhood, who finally came with a committee of his countryman to see what Hull House wanted of him, thoroughly convinced that no such effort could be disinterested. One dreary trial after another had been lost through the inadequacy of the existing legislation and after many attempts to secure better legal regulation of its sale a new law with the cooperation of many agencies was finally secured in 1907. Through all this the Italian druggist, who had greatly profited by the sale of cocaine to boys, only felt outraged and abused. And yet the thought of this campaign brings before my mind with irresistible force, a young Italian boy who died—a victim of the drug at the age of seventeen. He had been in our kindergarten as a handsome merry child, in our clubs as a vivacious boy, and then gradually there was an eclipse of all that was animated and joyous and promising, and when I at last saw him in his coffin, it was impossible to connect that haggard shriveled body with what I had known before.

A midwife investigation, undertaken in connection with the Chicago Medical Society, while showing the great need of further state regulation in the interest of the most ignorant mothers and helpless children, brought us into conflict with one of the most venerable of all customs. . . . Some of our investigations of course had no such untoward results, such as "An Intensive Study of Truancy" undertaken by a resident of Hull House in connection with the compulsory education department of the Board of Education and the Visiting Nurses Association. The resident, Mrs. Britton, who, having had charge of our children's clubs for many years, knew thousands of children in the neighborhood, made a detailed study of three hundred families tracing back the habitual truancy of the child to economic and social causes. This investigation preceded a most interesting conference on truancy held under a committee of which I was a member from the Chicago Board of Education. It left lasting results upon the administration of the truancy law as well as the cooperation of volunteer bodies.

We continually conduct small but careful investigations at Hull House, which may guide us in our immediate doings such as two recently undertaken by Mrs. Britton, one upon the reading of school children before new books were bought for the children's club libraries, and another on the proportion of tuberculosis among school children, before we opened a little experimental outdoor school on one of our balconies. Some of the Hull House investigations are purely negative in result; we once made an attempt to test the fatigue of factory girls in order to determine how far overwork superinduced the tuberculosis to which such a surprising number of them were victims. The one scientific instrument it seemed possible to use was an ergograph, a complicated and expensive instrument kindly lent to us from the physiological laboratory of the University of Chicago. I remember the imposing procession we made from Hull House to the factory full of working women, in which the proprietor allowed us to make the tests; first there was the precious instrument on a hand truck guarded by an anxious student and the young physician who was going to take the tests every afternoon; then there was Dr. Hamilton the resident in charge of the investigation, walking with a scientist who was interested to see that the instrument was properly installed; I followed in the rear to talk once more to the proprietor of the factory to be quite sure that he would permit the experiment to go on. The result of all this preparation, however, was to have the instrument record less fatigue at the end of the day than at the beginning, not because the girls had not worked hard and were not "dog tired" as they confessed, but because the instrument was not fitted to find it out.

For many years we have administered a branch station of the federal post office at Hull House, which we applied for in the first instance because our neighbors lost such a large percentage of the money they sent to Europe, through the commissions to middlemen. The experience in the post office constantly gave us data for urging the establishment of postal savings as we saw one perplexed immigrant after another turning away in bewilderment when he was told that the United States post office did not receive savings. . . .

The investigations of Hull House . . . tend to be merged with those of larger organizations, from the investigation of the social value of saloons made for the Committee of Fifty in 1896, to the one on infant mortality in relation to nationality, made for the American Academy of Science in 1909. . . .

Mr. Howells has said that we are all so besotted with our novel reading that we have lost the power of seeing certain aspects of life with any sense of reality because we are continually looking for the possible romance. The description might apply to the earlier years of the American settlement, but certainly the later years are filled with discoveries in actual life as romantic as they are unexpected. If I may illustrate one of these romantic discoveries from my own experience, I would cite the . . . internationalism . . . I have seen in our cosmopolitan neighborhood: when a South Italian Catholic is forced by the very exigencies of the situation to make friends with an Austrian Jew representing another nationality and another religion, both of which cut into all his most cherished prejudices, he . . . modifies his provincialism, for if an old enemy working by his side has turned into a friend, almost anything may happen. When, therefore, I became identified with the peace movement both in its International and National Conventions, I hoped that this internationalism engendered in the immigrant quarters of American cities might be recognized as an effective instrument in the cause of peace. I first set it forth with some misgiving before the Convention held in Boston in 1904 and it is always a pleasure to recall the hearty assent given to it by Professor William James.

I have always objected to the phrase "sociological laboratory" applied to us, because Settlements should be something much more human and spontaneous than such a phrase connotes, and yet it is inevitable that the residents should know their own neighborhoods more thoroughly than any other, and that their experiences there should affect their convictions.

Years ago I was much entertained by a story told at the Chicago Woman's Club by one of its ablest members in the discussion following a paper of mine on "The Outgrowths of Toynbee Hall." She said that when she was a little girl playing in her mother's garden, she one day discovered a small toad who seemed to her very forlorn and lonely, although she did not in the least know how to comfort him, she reluctantly left him to his fate; later in the day, quite at the other end of the garden, she found a large toad, also apparently without family and friends. With a heart full of tender sympathy, she took a stick and by exercising infinite patience and some skill, she finally pushed the little toad through the entire length of the garden into the company of the big toad, when, to her inexpressible horror and surprise, the big toad opened his mouth and swallowed the little one. The moral of the tale was clear applied to people who lived "where they did not naturally belong," although I protested that was exactly what we wanted—to be swallowed and digested, to disappear into the bulk of the people. . . .

Chapter Fourteen

Civic Cooperation

ONE OF THE first lessons we learned at Hull House was that private beneficence is totally inadequate to deal with the vast numbers of the city's disinherited. We also quickly came to realize that there are certain types of wretchedness from which every private philanthropy shrinks and which are cared for only in those wards of the county hospital provided for the wrecks of vicious living or in the city's isolation hospital for smallpox patients.

I have heard a broken-hearted mother exclaim when her erring daughter came home at last too broken and diseased to be taken into the family she had disgraced, "There is no place for her but the top floor of the County Hospital; they will have to take her there," and this only after every possible expedient had been tried or suggested. This aspect of governmental responsibility was unforgettably borne in upon me during the smallpox epidemic following the World's Fair, when one of the residents, Mrs. Kelley, as State Factory Inspector, was much concerned in discovering and destroying clothing which was being finished in houses containing unreported cases of smallpox. The deputy most successful in locating such cases lived at Hull House during the epidemic because he did not wish to expose his own family. Another resident, Miss Lathrop, as a member of the State Board of Charities, went back and forth to the crowded pest house which had been hastily constructed on a stretch of prairie west of the city. As Hull House was already so exposed, it seemed best for the special smallpox inspectors from the Board of Health to take their meals and change their clothing there before they went to their respective homes. All of these officials had accepted without question and as implicit in public office the obligation to carry on the dangerous and difficult undertakings for which private philanthropy is unfitted, as if the commonalty of compassion represented by the State was more comprehending than that of any individual group. . . .

In our first two summers we had maintained three baths in the basement of our own house for the use of the neighborhood, and they afforded some experience and argument for the erection of the first public bathhouse in Chicago, which was built on a neigh-boring street and opened under the city Board of Health. The lot upon which it was erected belonged to a friend of Hull House who offered it to the city without rent, and this enabled the city to erect the first public bath from the small appropriation of ten thousand dollars. Great fear was expressed by the public authorities that the baths would not be used, and the old story of the bathtubs in model tenements which had been turned into coal bins was often quoted to us. We were supplied, however, with the incontrovertible argument that in our adjacent third square mile there were in 1892 but three bathtubs and that this fact was much complained of by many of the tenement house dwellers. Our contention was justified by the immediate and overflowing use of the public baths, as we had before been sustained in the contention that an immigrant population would respond to opportunities for reading when the Public Library Board had established a branch reading room at Hull House.

We also quickly discovered that nothing brought us so absolutely into comradeship with our neighbors as mutual and sustained effort such as the paving of a street, the closing of a gambling house, or the restoration of a veteran police sergeant.

Several of these earlier attempts at civic cooperation were undertaken in connection with the Hull House

Men's Club, which had been organized in the spring of 1893, had been incorporated under a State charter of its own, and had occupied a clubroom in the gymnasium building. This club obtained an early success in one of the political struggles in the ward and thus fastened upon itself a specious reputation for political power.... Its early political success came in a campaign Hull House had instigated against a powerful alderman who has held office for more than twenty years in the nineteenth ward, and who, although notoriously corrupt, is still firmly entrenched among his constituents.

Hull House has had to do with three campaigns organized against him. In the first one he was apparently only amused at our "Sunday School" effort and did little to oppose the election to the aldermanic office of a member of the Hull House Men's Club who thus became his colleague in the city council. When Hull House, however, made an effort in the following spring against the re-election of the alderman himself, we encountered the most determined and skillful opposition. In these campaigns we doubtless depended too much upon the idealistic appeal for we did not yet comprehend the element of reality always brought into the political struggle in such a neighborhood where politics deal so directly with getting a job and earning a living.

We soon discovered that approximately one out of every five voters in the nineteenth ward at that time held a job dependent upon the good will of the alderman. There were no civil service rules to interfere, and the unskilled voter swept the street and dug the sewer, as secure in his position as the more sophisticated voter who tended a bridge or occupied an office chair in the city hall. The alderman was even more fortunate in finding places with the franchise-seeking corporations; it took us some time to understand why so large a proportion of our neighbors were streetcar employees and why we had such a large club composed solely of telephone girls. Our powerful alderman had various methods of entrenching himself. Many people were indebted to him for his kindly services in the police station and the justice courts, for in those days Irish constituents easily broke the peace, and before the establishment of the Juvenile Court, boys were arrested for very trivial offenses; added to these were hundreds of constituents indebted to him for personal kindness, from the peddler who received a free license to the businessman who had a railroad pass to New York. Our third campaign against him, when we succeeded in making a serious impression upon his majority, evoked from his henchmen the same sort of hostility which a striker so inevitably feels against the man who would take his job, even sharpened by the sense that the movement for reform came from an alien source.

Another result of the campaign was an expectation on the part of our new political friends that Hull

House would perform like offices for them, and there resulted endless confusion and misunderstanding because in many cases we could not even attempt to do what the alderman constantly did with a right good will. When he protected a lawbreaker from the legal consequences of his act, his kindness appeared, not only to himself but to all beholders, like the deed of a powerful and kindly statesman. When Hull House on the other hand insisted that a law must be enforced, it could but appear like the persecution of the offender. We were certainly not anxious for consistency nor for individual achievement, but in a desire to foster a higher political morality and not to lower our standards, we constantly clashed with the existing political code. We also unwittingly stumbled upon a powerful combination of which our alderman was the political head, with its banking, its ecclesiastical, and its journalistic representatives, and as we followed up the clue and naively told all we discovered, we of course laid the foundations for opposition which has manifested itself in many forms; the most striking expression of it was an attack upon Hull House lasting through weeks and months by a Chicago daily newspaper which has since ceased publication.

During the third campaign I received many anonymous letters—those from the men often obscene, those from the women revealing that curious connection between prostitution and the lowest type of politics which every city tries in vain to hide. I had offers from the men in the city prison to vote properly if released; various communications from lodging-house keepers as to the prices of the vote they were ready to deliver; everywhere appeared that animosity which is evoked only when a man feels that his means of livelihood is threatened. . . .

. . . These campaigns were not without their rewards; one of them was a quickened friendship both with the more substantial citizens in the ward and with a group of fine young voters whose devotion to Hull House has never since failed; another was a sense of identification with public-spirited men throughout the city who contributed money and time to what they considered a gallant effort against political corruption. I remember a young professor from the University of Chicago who with his wife came to live at Hull House, traveling the long distance everyday throughout the autumn and winter that he might qualify as a nineteenth-ward voter in the spring campaign. He served as a watcher at the polls and it was but a poor reward for his devotion that he was literally set upon and beaten up, for in those good old days such things frequently occurred. Many another case of devotion to our standard so recklessly raised might be cited, but perhaps more valuable than any of these was the sense of identification we obtained with the rest of Chicago.

So far as a Settlement can discern and bring to local consciousness neighborhood needs which are common needs, and can give vigorous help to the municipal measures through which such needs shall be met, it fulfills its most valuable function. To illustrate from our first effort to improve the street paving in the vicinity, we found that when we had secured the consent of the majority of the property owners on a given street for a new paving, the alderman checked the entire plan through his kindly service to one man who had appealed to him to keep the assessments down. The street long remained a shocking mass of wet, dilapidated cedar blocks, where children were sometimes mired as they floated a surviving block in the water which speedily filled the holes whence other blocks had been extracted for fuel. And yet when we were able to demonstrate that the street paving had thus been reduced into cedar pulp by the heavily loaded wagons of an adjacent factory, that the expense of its repaving should be borne from a general fund and not by the poor property owners, we found that we could all unite in advocating reform in the method of repaving assessments, and the alderman himself was obliged to come into such a popular movement. . . .

Certainly the need for civic cooperation was obvious in many directions, and in none more strikingly than in that organized effort which must be carried on unceasingly if young people are to be protected from the darker and coarser dangers of the city. The cooperation between Hull House and the Juvenile Protective Association came about gradually, and it seems now almost inevitably. From our earliest days we saw many boys constantly arrested, and I had a number of most enlightening experiences in the police station with an Irish lad whose mother upon her deathbed had begged me "to look after him." We were distressed by the gangs of very little boys who would sally forth with an enterprising leader in search of old brass and iron, sometimes breaking into empty houses for the sake of the faucets or lead pipe which they would sell for a good price to a junk dealer. With the money thus obtained they would buy cigarettes and beer or even candy, which could be conspicuously consumed in the alleys where they might enjoy the excitement of being seen and suspected by the "coppers." From the third year of Hull House, one of the residents held a semiofficial position in the nearest police station; at least, the sergeant agreed to give her provisional charge of every boy and girl under arrest for a trivial offense. . . .

It was not without hope that I might be able to forward in the public school system the solution of some of these problems of delinquency so dependent upon truancy and ill-adapted education that I became a member of the Chicago Board of Education in July 1905. . . .

. . . The appointment of seven new members, including myself, by Mayor Dunne was an epitome of the Mayor's . . . entire administration, which was founded upon the belief that if those citizens representing social ideals and reform principles were but appointed to office, public welfare must be established. . . .

. . . There had been a long effort of public school administration in America to free itself from the rule and exploitation of politics. In every city for many years the politician had secured positions for his friends as teachers and janitors; he had received a rake-off in the contract for every new building or coal supply or adoption of schoolbooks. In the long struggle against this political corruption, the one remedy continually advocated was the transfer of authority in all educational matters from the Board to the superintendent. The one cure for "pull" and corruption was the authority of the "expert." The rules and records of the Chicago Board of Education are full of relics of this long struggle honestly waged by honest men, who unfortunately became content with the ideals of an "efficient business administration." These businessmen established an able superintendent with a large salary, with his tenure of office secured by State law so that he would not be disturbed by the wrath of the balked politician. They instituted impersonal examinations for the teachers both as to entrance into the system and promotion, and they proceeded "to hold the superintendent responsible" for smooth-running schools. All this, however, dangerously approximated the commercialistic ideal of high salaries only for the management with the final test of a small expense account and a large output.

In this long struggle for a quarter of a century to free the public schools from political interference, in Chicago at least, the high wall of defense erected around the school system in order "to keep the rascals out" unfortunately so restricted the teachers inside the system that they had no space in which to move about freely and the more adventurous of them fairly panted for light and air. Any attempt to lower the wall for the sake of the teachers within was regarded as giving an opportunity to the politicians without, and they were often openly accused, with a show of truth, of being in league with each other. Whenever the minority Dunne members of the Board attempted to secure more liberty for the teachers, we were warned by tales of former difficulties with the politicians. . . .

I certainly played a most inglorious part in this unnecessary conflict; I was chairman of the School Management Committee during one year when a majority of the members seemed to me exasperatingly conservative, and during another year when they were frustratingly radical, and I was of course highly unsatisfactory to both. Certainly a plan to retain the undoubted benefit of required study for teachers in such wise as to lessen its burden, and various schemes devised to shift the emphasis from scholarship to professional work, were mostly impatiently repudiated by the Teachers' Federation, and when one badly mutilated plan finally passed the Board, it was most reluctantly administered by the superintendent. . . .

It is difficult to close this chapter without a reference to the efforts made in Chicago to secure the municipal franchise for women. During two long periods of agitation for a new city charter, a representative body of women appealed to the public, to the charter convention, and to the Illinois legislature for this very reasonable provision. During the campaign when I acted as chairman of the federation of a hundred women's organizations, nothing impressed me so forcibly as the fact that the response came from bodies of women representing the most varied traditions. We were joined by a church society of hundreds of Lutheran women, because Scandinavian women had exercised the municipal franchise since the seventeenth century and had found American cities strangely conservative; by organizations of working women who had keenly felt the need of the municipal franchise in order to secure for their workshops the most rudimentary sanitation and the consideration which the vote alone obtains for workingmen; by federations of mothers' meetings, who were interested in clean

milk and the extension of kindergartens; by prop-
erty-owning women, who had been powerless to
protest against unjust taxation; by organizations of
professional women, of university students, and of
collegiate alumnae; and by women's clubs interested
in municipal reforms. There was a complete absence
of the traditional women's rights clamor, but much
impressive testimony from busy and useful women
that they had reached the place where they needed
the franchise in order to carry on their own affairs.

A striking witness as to the need of the ballot, even
for the women who are restricted to the most primitive and traditional activities, occurred when some
Russian women waited upon me to ask whether under
the new charter they could vote for covered markets
and so get rid of the shocking Chicago grime upon
all their food; and when some neighboring Italian
women sent me word that they would certainly vote
for public washhouses if they ever had the chance to
vote at all. It was all so human, so spontaneous, and
so direct that it really seemed as if the time must be
ripe for political expression of that public concern on
the part of women which had so long been forced to
seek indirection. None of these busy women wished
to take the place of men or to influence them in the
direction of men's affairs, but they did seek an opportunity to cooperate directly in civic life through the
use of the ballot in regard to their own affairs. . . .

Chapter Fifteen

The Value of Social Clubs

F ROM THE EARLY days at Hull House, social
clubs composed of English-speaking Ameri-
can-born young people grew apace. So eager
were they for social life that no mistakes in management could drive them away. I remember one enthusiastic leader who read aloud to a club a translation of
Antigone, which she had selected because she believed
that the great themes of the Greek poets were best
suited to young people. She came into the clubroom
one evening in time to hear the president call the
restive members to order with the statement, "You
might just as well keep quiet for she is bound to finish it, and the quicker she gets to reading, the longer
time we'll have for dancing." And yet the same club
leader had the pleasure of lending four copies of the

drama to four of the members, and one young man almost literally committed the entire play to memory.

On the whole we were much impressed by the great desire for self-improvement, for study and debate, exhibited by many of the young men. This very tendency, in fact, brought one of the most promising of our earlier clubs to an untimely end. The young men in the club, twenty in number, had grown much irritated by the frivolity of the girls during their long debates, and had finally proposed that three of the most "frivolous" be expelled. Pending a final vote, the three culprits appealed to certain of their friends who were members of the Hull House Men's Club, between whom and the debating young men the incident became the cause of a quarrel so bitter that at length it led to a shooting. Fortunately the shot missed fire, or it may have been true that it was "only intended for a scare," but at any rate, we were all thoroughly frightened by this manifestation of the hot blood which the defense of woman has so often evoked.

After many efforts to bring about a reconciliation, the debating club of twenty young men and the seventeen young women, who either were or pretended to be sober minded, rented a hall a mile west of Hull House severing their connection with us because their ambitious and right-minded efforts had been unappreciated, basing this on the ground that we had not urged the expulsion of the so-called "tough" members of the Men's Club, who had been involved in the difficulty. The seceding club invited me to the first meeting in their new quarters that I might present to them my version of the situation and set forth the incident from the standpoint of Hull House. The discussion I had with the young people that evening has always remained with me as one of the moments of illumination which life in a Settlement so often affords. In response to my position that a desire to avoid all that was "tough" meant to walk only in the paths of smug self-seeking and personal improvement leading straight into the pit of self-righteousness and petty achievement and was exactly what the Settlement did not stand for, they contended with much justice that ambitious young people were obliged for their own reputation, if not for their own morals, to avoid all connection with that which bordered on the tough, and that it was quite another matter for the Hull House residents who could afford a more generous judgment. It was in vain I urged that life teaches us nothing more inevitably than that right and wrong are most confusingly confounded; that the blackest wrong may be within our own motives, and that at the best, right will not dazzle us by its radiant shining and can only be found by exerting patience and discrimination. They still maintained their wholesome bourgeois position, which I am now quite ready to admit was most reasonable.

Of course there were many disappointments connected with these clubs when the rewards of political and commercial life easily drew the members away from the principles advocated in club meetings. One of the young men who had been a shining light in the advocacy of municipal reform deserted in the middle of a reform campaign because he had been offered a lucrative office in the city hall; another even after a course of lectures on business morality, "worked" the club itself to secure orders for custom-made clothing from samples of cloth he displayed, although the orders were filled by ready-made suits slightly refitted and delivered at double their original price. But nevertheless, there was much to cheer us as we gradually became acquainted with the daily living of the vigorous young men and women who filled to overflowing all the social clubs.

. . . Having lived in a Settlement twenty years, I see scores of young people who have successfully established themselves in life and in my travels in the city and outside, I am constantly cheered by greetings from the rising young lawyer, the scholarly rabbi, the successful teacher, the prosperous young matron buying clothes for blooming children. "Don't you remember me? I used to belong to a Hull House club." I once asked one of these young people, a man who held a good position on a Chicago daily, what special thing Hull House had meant to him, and he promptly replied, "It was the first house I had ever been in where books and magazines just lay around as if there were plenty of them in the world. Don't you remember how much I used to read at that little round table at the back of the library? To have people regard reading as a reasonable occupation changed the whole aspect of life to me and I began to have confidence in what I could do."

. . . One supreme gaiety has come to be an annual event of such importance that it is talked of from year to year. For six weeks before St. Patrick's Day, a small group of residents put their best powers of invention and construction into preparation for a cotillion which is like a pageant in its gaiety and vigor. The parents sit in the gallery, and the mothers appreciate more than anyone else perhaps, the value of this ball to which an invitation is so highly prized; although their standards of manners may differ widely from the conventional, they know full well when the companionship of the young people is safe and unsullied. . . .

Although . . . conventional customs are carefully enforced at our many parties and festivities, and while the dancing classes are as highly prized for the opportunity they afford for enforcing standards as for their ostensible aim, the residents at Hull House, in their efforts to provide opportunities for clean recreation, receive the most valued help from the experienced wisdom of the older women of the neighborhood.

Bowen Hall is constantly used for dancing parties with soft drinks established in its foyer. The parties given by the Hull House clubs are by invitation and the young people themselves carefully maintain their standard of entrance so that the most cautious mother may feel safe when her daughter goes to one of our parties. No club festivity is permitted without the presence of a director; no young man under the influence of liquor is allowed; certain types of dancing often innocently started are strictly prohibited; and above all, early closing is insisted upon. This standardizing of pleasure has always seemed an obligation to the residents of Hull House, but we are, I hope, saved from that priggishness which young people so heartily resent, by the Mardi Gras dance and other festivities which the residents themselves arrange and successfully carry out.

In spite of our belief that the standards of a ball may be almost as valuable to those without as to those within, the residents are constantly concerned for those many young people in the neighborhood who are too hedonistic to submit to the discipline of a dancing class or even to the claim of a pleasure club, but who go about in freebooter fashion to find pleasure wherever it may be cheaply on sale.

Such young people, well meaning but impatient of control, become the easy victims of the worst type of public dance halls, and of even darker places, whose purposes are hidden under music and dancing. We were thoroughly frightened when we learned that during the year which ended last December, more than twenty-five thousand young people under the age of twenty-five passed through the Juvenile and Municipal Courts of Chicago—approximately one out of every eighty of the entire population, or one out of every fifty-two of those under twenty-five years of age. One's heart aches for these young people caught by the outside glitter of city gaiety, who make such a feverish attempt to snatch it for themselves. The young people in our clubs are comparatively safe, but many instances come to the knowledge of Hull House residents which make us long for the time when the city, through more small parks, municipal gymnasiums, and schoolrooms open for recreation, can guard from disaster these young people who walk so carelessly on the edge of the pit. . . .

That more . . . girls do not come to grief is due to those mothers who understand the insatiable demand for a good time, and if all of the mothers did understand, those pathetic statistics which show that four fifths of all prostitutes are under twenty years of age would be marvelously changed. We are told that "the will to live" is aroused in each baby by his mother's irresistible desire to play with him, the physiological value of joy that a child is born, and that the high death rate in institutions is increased by "the discontented babies" whom no one persuades into living. Something of the same sort is necessary in that second birth at adolescence. The young people need affection and understanding each one for himself, if they are to be induced to live in an inheritance of decorum and safety and to understand the foundations upon which this orderly world rests. No one comprehends their needs so sympathetically as those mothers who iron the flimsy starched finery of their grown-up daughters late into the night, and who pay for a red velvet parlor set on the installment plan, although the younger children may sadly need new shoes. These mothers apparently understand the sharp demand for social pleasure and do their best to respond to it, although at the same time they constantly minister to all the physical needs of an exigent family of little children. We often come to a realization of the truth of Walt Whitman's statement, that one of the surest sources of wisdom is the mother of a large family.

It is but natural, perhaps, that the members of the Hull House Woman's Club whose prosperity has given them some leisure and a chance to remove their own families to neighborhoods less full of temptations, should have offered their assistance in our attempt to provide recreation for these restless young people. In many instances their experience in the club itself has enabled them to perceive these needs. One day a Juvenile Court officer told me that a woman's club member, who has a large family of her own and one boy sufficiently difficult, had undertaken to care for a ward of the Juvenile Court who lived only a block from her house, and that she had kept him in the path of rectitude for six months. In reply to my congratulations upon this successful bit of reform to the club woman herself, she said that she was quite ashamed that she had not undertaken the task earlier for she had for years known the boy's mother who scrubbed a downtown office building, leaving home every evening at five and returning at eleven during the very time the boy could most easily find opportunities for wrongdoing. She said that her obligation toward this boy had not occurred to her until one day when the club members were making pillowcases for the Detention Home of the Juvenile Court, it suddenly seemed perfectly obvious that her share in the salvation of wayward children was to care for this particular boy and she had asked the Juvenile Court officer to commit him to her. She invited the boy to her house to supper everyday that she might know just where he was at the crucial moment of twilight, and she adroitly managed to keep him under her own roof for the evening if she did not approve of the plans he had made. . . .

Very early in its history the Hull House Woman's Club formed what was called "A Social Extension

Committee." Once a month this committee gives parties to people in the neighborhood who for any reason seem forlorn and without much social pleasure. One evening they invited only Italian women, thereby crossing a distinct social "gulf," for there certainly exists as great a sense of social difference between the prosperous Irish-American women and the South-Italian peasants as between any two sets of people in the city of Chicago. The Italian women, who were almost eastern in their habits, all stayed at home and sent their husbands, and the social extension committee entered the drawing room to find it occupied by rows of Italian workingmen, who seemed to prefer to sit in chairs along the wall. They were quite ready to be "socially extended," but plainly puzzled as to what it was all about. The evening finally developed into a very successful party, not so much because the committee were equal to it, as because the Italian men rose to the occasion.

Untiring pairs of them danced the tarantella; they sang Neapolitan songs; one of them performed some of those wonderful sleight-of-hand tricks so often seen on the streets of Naples; they explained the coral finger of St. Januarius which they wore; they politely ate the strange American refreshments; and when the evening was over, one of the committee said to me, "Do you know I am ashamed of the way I have always talked about 'dagos,' they are quite like other people, only one must take a little more pains with them. . . ." We send our young people to Europe that they may lose their provincialism and be able to judge their fellows by a more universal test, as we send them to college that they may attain the cultural background and a larger outlook; all of these it is possible to acquire in other ways, as this member of the woman's club had discovered for herself.

This social extension committee under the leadership of an ex-president of the Club, a Hull House resident with a wide acquaintance, also discovers many of those lonely people of which every city contains so large a number. We are only slowly apprehending the very real danger to the individual who fails to establish some sort of genuine relation with the people who surround him. We are all more or less familiar with the results of isolation in rural districts; the Bronte sisters have portrayed the hideous immorality and savagery of the remote dwellers on the bleak moorlands of northern England; . . . but tales still wait to be told of the isolated city dweller. . . .

Many instances of this come into my mind; the faded, ladylike hairdresser, who came and went to her work for twenty years, carefully concealing her dwelling place from the "other people in the shop," moving whenever they seemed too curious about it, and priding herself that no neighbor had ever "stepped inside her door," and yet when discovered through an asthma which forced her to crave friendly offices, she was most responsive and even gay in a social atmosphere. Another woman made a long effort to conceal the poverty resulting from her husband's inveterate gambling and to secure for her children the educational advantages to which her family had always been accustomed. Her five children, who are now university graduates, do not realize how hard and solitary was her early married life when we first knew her, and she was beginning to regret the isolation in which her children were being reared, for she saw that their lack of early companionship would always cripple their power to make friends. She was glad to avail herself of the social resources of Hull House for them and at last even for herself.

The leader of the social extension committee has also been able, through her connection with the vacant lot garden movement in Chicago, to maintain a most flourishing "friendly club" largely composed of people who cultivate these garden plots. . . . Their jollity and enthusiasm are unbounded, expressing itself in clog dances and rousing old songs often in sharp contrast to the overworked, worn aspects of the members. . . .

Chapter Sixteen

Arts at Hull House

THE FIRST BUILDING erected for Hull House contained an art gallery well lighted for day and evening use, and our first exhibit of loaned pictures was opened in June 1891, by Mr. and Mrs. Barnett of London. It is always pleasant to associate their hearty sympathy with that first exhibit, and thus to connect it with their pioneer efforts at Toynbee Hall to secure for working people the opportunity to know the best art, and with their establishment of the first permanent art gallery in an industrial quarter.

We took pride in the fact that our first exhibit contained some of the best pictures Chicago afforded, and we conscientiously insured them against fire and carefully guarded them by night and day. . . .

The loan exhibits were continued until the Chicago Art Institute was opened free to the public on Sunday afternoons and parties were arranged at Hull House and conducted there by a guide. In time even these parties were discontinued as the galleries became better known in all parts of the city and the Art Institute management did much to make pictures popular. . . .

Miss Starr at length found herself quite impatient with her role of lecturer on the arts, while all the handicraft about her was untouched by beauty and did not even reflect the interest of the workman. She took a training in bookbinding in London under Mr. Cobden-Sanderson and established her bindery at Hull House in which design and workmanship, beauty and thoroughness are taught to a small number of apprentices.

From the very first winter, concerts which are still continued were given every Sunday afternoon in the Hull House drawing room and later, as the audiences increased, in the larger halls. For these we are indebted to musicians from every part of the city. . . .

The recitals and concerts given by the Hull House Music School are attended by large and appreciative audiences. On the Sunday before Christmas the program of Christmas songs draws together people of the most diverging faiths. In the deep tones of the memorial organ erected at Hull House, we realize that music is perhaps the most potent agent for making the universal appeal and inducing men to forget their differences.

Some of the pupils in the music school have developed during the years into trained musicians and are supporting themselves in their chosen profession. On the other hand, we constantly see the most promising musical ability extinguished when the young people enter industries which so sap their vitality that they cannot carry on serious study in the scanty hours outside of factory work. . . .

. . . Sometimes bitter experience did not prepare us for the sorrowful year when six promising pupils out of a class of fifteen, developed tuberculosis. It required but little penetration to see that during the eight years the class of fifteen schoolchildren had come together to the music school, they had approximately an even chance, but as soon as they reached the legal working age only a scanty moiety of those who became self-supporting could endure the strain of long hours and bad air. . . .

The universal desire for the portrayal of life lying quite outside of personal experience evinces itself in many forms. One of the conspicuous features of our neighborhood, as of all industrial quarters, is the persistency with which the entire population attends the theater. . . .

There were two young girls whose sober parents did not approve of the theater and would allow no money for such foolish purposes. In sheer desperation the sisters evolved a plot that one of them would feign a toothache, and while she was having her tooth pulled by a neighboring dentist the other would steal the gold crowns from his table, and with the money thus procured they could attend the vaudeville theater every night on their way home from work. Apparently the pain and wrongdoing did not weigh for a moment against the anticipated pleasure. The plan was carried out to the point of selling the gold crowns to a pawnbroker when the disappointed girls were arrested. . . .

Long before the Hull House theater was built we had many plays, first in the drawing room and later in the gymnasium. The young people's clubs never tired of rehearsing and preparing for these dramatic occasions, and we also discovered that older people were almost equally ready and talented. We quickly learned that no celebration at Thanksgiving was so popular as a graphic portrayal on the stage of the Pilgrim Fathers, and we were often put to it to reduce to dramatic effects the great days of patriotism and religion. . . .

. . . Every year at the Hull House annual exhibition, . . . an effort is made to bring together in a spirit of holiday the nine thousand people who come to the House every week during duller times. Curiously enough the central feature at the annual exhibition seems to be the brass band of the boys' club which apparently dominates the situation by sheer size and noise. . . .

Chapter Seventeen

Echoes of the Russian Revolution

I**N THE** ... wonderful procession of revolutionists, Prince Kropotkin, or, as he prefers to be called, Peter Kropotkin, was doubtless the most distinguished. When he came to America to lecture, he was heard throughout the country with great interest and respect; that he was a guest of Hull House during his stay in Chicago attracted little attention at the time, but two years later, when the assassination of President McKinley occurred, the visit of this kindly scholar, who had always called himself an "anarchist" and had certainly written fiery tracts in his younger manhood, was made the basis of an attack upon Hull House by a daily newspaper, which ignored the fact that while Prince Kropotkin had addressed the Chicago Arts and Crafts Society at Hull House, giving a digest of his remarkable book on *Fields, Factories, and Workshops*, he had also spoken at the State Universities of Illinois and Wisconsin and before the leading literary and scientific societies of Chicago. These institutions and societies were not, therefore, called anarchistic. Hull House had doubtless laid itself open to this attack through an incident connected with the imprisonment of the editor on an anarchistic paper, who was arrested in Chicago immediately after the assassination of President McKinley. In the excitement following the national calamity and the avowal by the assassin of the influence of the anarchistic lecture to which he had listened, arrests were made in Chicago of every one suspected of anarchy, in the belief that a widespread plot would be uncovered. The editor's house was searched for incriminating literature, his wife and daughter taken to a police station, and his son and himself, with several other suspected anarchists, were placed in the disused cells in the basement of the city hall.

. . . The group of wretched men detained in the old-fashioned, scarcely habitable cells, had not the least idea of their ultimate fate. They were not allowed to see an attorney and were kept "incommunicado" as their excited friends called it. I had seen the editor and his family only during Prince Kropotkin's stay at

Hull House, when they had come to visit him several times. The editor had impressed me as a quiet, scholarly man, challenging the social order by the philosophic touchstone of Bakunin and of Herbert Spencer, somewhat startled by the radicalism of his fiery young son and much comforted by the German domesticity of his wife and daughter. Perhaps it was but my hysterical symptom of the universal excitement, but it certainly seemed to me more than I could bear when a group of his individualistic friends, who had come to ask for help, said: "You see what becomes of your boasted law; the authorities won't even allow an attorney, nor will they accept bail for these men, against whom nothing can be proved, although the veriest criminals are not denied such a right." Challenged by an anarchist, one is always sensitive for the honor of legally constituted society, and I replied that of course the men could have an attorney, that the assassin himself would eventually be furnished with one, that the fact that a man was an anarchist had nothing to do with his rights before the law! I was met with the retort that that might do for a theory, but that the fact still remained that these men had been absolutely isolated, seeing no one but policemen, who constantly frightened them with tales of public clamor and threatened lynching.

The conversation took place on Saturday night and, as the final police authority rests in the mayor, with a friend who was equally disturbed over the situation, I repaired to his house on Sunday morning to appeal to him in the interest of a law and order that should not yield to panic. We contended that to the anarchist above all men it must be demonstrated that law is impartial and stands the test of every strain. The mayor heard us through with the ready sympathy of the successful politician. He insisted, however, that the men thus far had merely been properly protected against lynching, but that it might now be safe to allow them to see someone; he would not yet, however, take the responsibility of permitting an attorney, but if I myself chose to see them on the humanitarian errand of an assurance of fair play, he would write me a permit at once. I promptly fell into the trap, if trap it was, and within half an hour was in a corridor in the city hall basement, talking to the distracted editor and surrounded by a cordon of police, who assured me that it was not safe to permit him out of his cell. The editor, who had grown thin and haggard under his suspense, asked immediately as to the whereabouts of his wife and daughter, concerning whom he had heard not a word since he had seen them arrested. Gradually he became composed as he learned, not that his testimony had been believed to the effect that he had never seen the assassin but once and had then considered him a foolish half-witted creature, but that the most thoroughgoing "dragnet" investigations on the part of the united police of the country had failed to discover a plot and that the public was gradually becoming convinced that the dastardly act was that of a solitary man with no political or social affiliations.

The entire conversation was simple and did not seem to me unlike, in motive or character, interviews I had had with many another forlorn man who had fallen into prison. I had scarce returned to Hull House, however, before it was filled with reporters, and I at once discovered that whether or not I had helped a brother out of a pit, I had fallen into a deep one myself. A period of sharp public opprobrium followed, traces of which, I suppose, will always remain. And yet in the midst of the letters of protest and accusation which made my mail a horror every morning came a few letters of another sort, one from a federal judge whom I had never seen and another from a distinguished professor in the constitutional law, who congratulated me on what they termed a sane attempt to uphold the law in time of panic. . . .

It seemed to me then that in the millions of words uttered and written at that time, no one adequately urged that public-spirited citizens set themselves the task of patiently discovering how these sporadic acts of violence against government may be understood and averted. We do not know whether they occur among the discouraged and unassimilated immigrants who might be cared for in such a way as enormously to lessen the probability of these acts, or whether they are the result of anarchistic teaching. By hastily concluding that the latter is the sole explanation for them, we make no attempt to heal and cure the situation. Failure to make a proper diagnosis may mean treatment of a disease which does not exist, or it may furthermore mean that the dire malady from which the patient is suffering be permitted to develop unchecked. And yet as the details of the meager life of the President's assassin were disclosed, they were a challenge to the forces for social betterment in American cities. Was it not an indictment to all those whose business it is to interpret and solace the wretched, that a boy should have grown up in an American city so uncared for, so untouched by higher issues, his wounds of life so unhealed by religion that the first talk he ever heard dealing with life's wrongs, although anarchistic and violent, should yet appear to point a way of relief? . . .

In the midst of his remorse, the cobbler told me a tale of his own youth; that years before, when an ardent young fellow in Germany, newly converted to the philosophy of anarchism, as he called it, he had made up his mind that the Church, as much as the State, was responsible for human oppression, and that this fact could best be set forth "in the deed" by the public destruction of a clergyman or priest; that he had carried firearms for a year with this purpose in mind, but that one pleasant summer evening, in a moment of weakness, he had confided his intention to a friend, and that from that moment he not only lost all desire to carry it out, but it seemed to him the most preposterous thing imaginable. In concluding the story he said; "That poor fellow sat just beside me on my bench; if I had only put my hand on his shoulder and said, 'Now, look here, brother, what is on your mind? What makes you talk such nonsense? Tell me. I have seen much of life, and understand all kinds of men. I have been young and hot-headed and foolish myself,' if he had told me of his purpose then and there, he would never have carried it out. The whole nation would have been spared this horror." As he concluded he shook his gray head and sighed as if the whole incident were more than he could bear—one of those terrible sins of omission; one of the things he "ought to have done," the memory of which is so hard to endure. . . .

. . . Hull House again became associated with . . . "foreign anarchists" six years later. This again was an echo of the Russian revolution, but in connection with one of its humblest representatives. A young Russian Jew named Averbuch appeared in the early morning at the house of the Chicago chief of police upon an obscure errand. It was a moment of panic everywhere in regard to anarchists because of a recent murder in Denver which had been charged to an Italian anarchist, and the chief of police, assuming that the dark young man standing in his hallway was an anarchist bent upon his assassination, hastily called for help. In a panic born of fear and self-defense, young Averbuch was shot to death. . . . The police might be right or wrong in their assertion that the man was an anarchist. It was, to our minds, also most unfortunate that the Chicago police in their determination to uncover an anarchistic plot should have utilized the most drastic methods of search within the Russian-Jewish colony composed of families only too familiar with the methods of Russian police. Therefore, when the Chicago police ransacked all the printing offices they could locate in the colony, when they raided a restaurant which they regarded as suspicious because it had been supplying food at cost to the unemployed, when they searched through private houses for papers and photographs of revolutionaries, when they seized the library of the Edelstadt group and carried the books, including Shakespeare and Herbert Spencer, to the city hall, when they arrested two friends of young Averbuch and kept them in the police station forty-eight hours, when they mercilessly "sweated" the sister, Olga, that she might be startled into a confession—all these things so poignantly reminded them of Russian methods that indignation fed both by old memory and bitter disappointment in America, swept over the entire colony. . . .

The belief of many Russians that the Averbuch incident would be made a prelude to the constant use of the extradition treaty for the sake of terrorizing revolutionists both at home and abroad received a certain corroboration when an attempt was made in 1908 to extradite a Russian revolutionist named Rudovitz who was living in Chicago. The first hearing before a United States Commissioner gave a verdict favorable to the Russian Government although this was afterward reversed by the Department of State in Washington. Partly to educate American sentiment, partly to express sympathy with the Russian refugees in their dire need, a series of public meetings was arranged in which the operations of the extradition treaty were discussed by many of us who had spoken at a meeting held in protest against its ratification fifteen years before. It is impossible for anyone unacquainted with the Russian colony to realize the consternation produced by this attempted extradition. I acted as treasurer of the fund collected to defray the expenses of halls and printing in the campaign against the policy of extradition and had many opportunities to talk with members of the colony. One old man, tearing his hair and beard as he spoke, declared that all his sons and grandsons might thus be sent back to Russia; in fact, all of the younger men in the colony might be extradited, for every high-spirited young Russian was, in a sense, a revolutionist.

Would it not provoke to ironic laughter that very nemesis which presides over the destinies of nations, if the most autocratic government yet remaining in civilization* should succeed in utilizing for its own autocratic methods the youngest and most daring experiment in democratic government which the world has ever seen? Stranger results have followed a course of stupidity and injustice resulting from blindness and panic! . . .

Thus a Settlement becomes involved in the many difficulties of its neighbors as its experiences make vivid the consciousness of modern internationalism. And yet the very fact that the sense of reality is so keen and the obligation of the Settlement so obvious may perhaps in itself explain the opposition Hull House has encountered when it expressed its sympathy with the Russian revolution. We were much entertained, although somewhat ruefully, when a Chicago woman withdrew from us a large annual subscription because Hull House had defended a Russian refugee while she, who had seen much of the Russian aristocracy in Europe, knew from them that all the revolutionary agitation was both unreasonable and unnecessary! . . .

---

* The Czar's government of Russia before the Revolution.

Chapter Eighteen
Socialized Education

T HE TEACHER IN a Settlement is constantly put upon his mettle to discover methods of instruction which shall make knowledge quickly available to his pupils, and I should like here to pay my tribute of admiration to the dean of our educational department, Miss Landsberg, and to the many men and women who every winter come regularly to Hull House, putting untiring energy into the endless task of teaching the newly arrived immigrant the first use of a language of which he has such desperate need. Even a meager knowledge of English may mean an opportunity to work in a factory *versus* nonemployment, or it may mean a question of life or death when a sharp command must be understood in order to avoid the danger of a descending crane.

In response to a demand for an education which should be immediately available, classes have been established and grown apace in cooking, dressmaking, and millinery. A girl who attends them will often say that she "expects to marry a workingman next spring," and because she has worked in a factory so long she knows "little about a house." Sometimes classes are composed of young matrons of like factory experiences. I recall one of them whose husband had become so desperate after two years of her unskilled cooking that he had threatened to desert her and go where he could get "decent food," as she confided to me in a tearful interview, when she followed my advice to take the Hull House courses in cooking, and at the end of six months reported a united and happy home.

Two distinct trends are found in response to these classes; the first is for domestic training, and the other is for trade teaching which shall enable the poor little milliner and dressmaker apprentices to shorten the years of errand running which is supposed to teach them their trade.

The beginning of trade instruction has been already evolved in connection with the Hull House Boys' Club. The ample Boys' Club building presented to Hull House three years ago by one of our trustees has afforded well-equipped shops for work in wood, iron, and brass; for smithing in copper and tin; for commercial photography, for printing, for telegraphy, and electrical construction. These shops have been filled with boys who are eager for that which seems to give them a clue to the industrial life all about them. These classes meet twice a week and are taught by intelligent workingmen who apparently give the boys what they want better than do the strictly professional teachers. While these classes in no sense provide a trade training, they often enable a boy to discover his aptitude and help him in the selection of what he "wants to be" by reducing the trades to embryonic forms. . . .

Out of the fifteen hundred members of the Hull House Boy's Club, hundreds seem to respond only to the opportunities for recreation, and many of the older ones apparently care only for the bowling and the billiards. And yet tournaments and match games under supervision and regulated hours are a great advance over the sensual and exhausting pleasures to be found so easily outside the club. These organized sports readily connect themselves with the Hull House gymnasium and with all those enthusiasms which are so mysteriously aroused by athletics.

Our gymnasium has been filled with large and enthusiastic classes for eighteen years in spite of the popularity of dancing and other possible substitutes, while the Saturday evening athletic contests have become a feature of the neighborhood. The Settlement strives for that type of gymnastics which is at least partly a matter of character, for that training which presupposes abstinence and the curbing of impulse, as well as for those athletic contests in which the mind of the contestant must be vigilant to keep the body closely to the rules of the game. . . .

It was in connection with a large association of Greek lads that Hull House finally lifted its long restriction against military drill. If athletic contests are the residuum of warfare first waged against the conqueror without and then against the tyrants within the State, the modern Greek youth is still in the first stage so far as his inherited attitude against the Turk is concerned. Each lad believes that at any moment he may be called home to fight this longtime enemy of Greece. With such a genuine motive at hand, it seemed mere affectation to deny the use of our boys' club building and gymnasium for organized drill, although happily it forms but a small part of the activities of the Greek Educational Association.

Having thus confessed to military drill countenanced if not encouraged at Hull House, it is perhaps only fair to relate an early experience of mine with the "Columbian Guards," and organization of the World's Fair summer. Although the Hull House squad was organized as the others were with the motto of a clean city, it was very anxious for military drill. This request not only shocked my nonresistant principles, but seemed to afford an opportunity to find a substitute for the military tactics which were used in the boys' brigades everywhere, even in those connected with churches. As the cleaning of the filthy streets and alleys was the ostensible purpose of the Columbian guards, I suggested to the boys that we work out a drill with sewer spades, which with their long narrow blades and shortened handles were not so unlike bayoneted guns in size, weight, and general appearance, but that much of the usual military drill could be readapted. While I myself was present at the gymnasium to explain that it was nobler to drill in imitation of removing disease-breeding filth than to drill in simulation of warfare; while I distractedly readapted tales of chivalry to this modern rescuing of the endangered and distressed, the new drill went forward in some sort of fashion, but so surely as I withdrew, the drillmaster would complain that our troops would first grow self-conscious, then demoralized, and finally flatly refuse to go on. Throughout the years since the failure of this quixotic experiment, I occasionally find one of these sewer spades in a Hull House storeroom, too truncated to be used for its original purpose and too prosaic to serve the purpose for which it was bought. I can only look at it in the forlorn hope that it may foreshadow that piping time when the weapons of warfare shall be turned into the implements of civic salvation.

Before closing this chapter on Socialized Education, it is only fair to speak of the education accruing to the Hull House residents themselves during their years of living in what at least purports to be a center for social and educational activity.

While a certain number of the residents are primarily interested in charitable administration and the amelioration which can be suggested only by those who know actual conditions, there are other residents identified with the House from its earlier years to whom the groups of immigrants make the historic appeal, and who use, not only their linguistic ability, but all the resource they can command of travel and reading to qualify themselves for intelligent living in the immigrant quarter of the city. . . .

There is no doubt that residents in a Settlement too often move toward their ends "with hurried and ignoble gait," putting forth thorns in their eagerness to bear grapes. It is always easy for those in pursuit of ends which they consider of overwhelming importance to become themselves thin and impoverished in spirit and temper, to gradually develop a dark mistaken eagerness alternating with fatigue, which supersedes "the great and gracious ways" so much more congruous with worthy aims. . . .

It may not be true "That the good are always the merry / Save by an evil chance," but a Settlement would make clear that one need not be heartless and flippant in order to be merry, nor solemn in order to be wise. Therefore quite as Hull House tries to redeem billiard tables from the association of gambling, and dancing from the temptations of the public dance halls, so it would associate with a life of upright purpose those more engaging qualities which in the experience of the neighborhood are too often connected with dubious aims.

Throughout the history of Hull House many inquiries have been made concerning the religion of the residents, and the reply that they are as diversified in belief and in the ardor of the inner life as any like number of people in a college or similar group, apparently does not carry conviction. I recall that after a house for men residents had been opened on Polk Street and the residential force at Hull House numbered twenty, we made an effort to come together on Sunday evenings in a household service, hoping thus to express our moral unity in spite of the fact that we represented many creeds. But although all of us reverently knelt when the High Church resident read the evening service and bowed our heads when the evangelical resident led in prayer after his chapter, and although we sat respectfully through the twilight when a resident read her favorite passages from Plato and another from Abt Vogler, we concluded at the end of the winter that . . . there were among us Jews, Roman Catholics, English Churchmen, Dissenters, and a few agnostics, and . . .

we . . . found unsatisfactory the diluted form of wor-
ship which we could carry on together. . . .

. . . Our Settlement has gathered into residence
people of widely diversified tastes and interests, and
. . . the group has been surprisingly permanent. The
majority of the present corp of forty residents support themselves by their business and professional
occupations in the city, giving only their leisure time
to Settlement undertakings. This in itself tends to
continuity of residence and has certain advantages.
Among the present staff, of whom the larger number
have been in residence for more than twelve years,
there are the secretary of the City Club, two practicing physicians, several attorneys, newspapermen,
businessmen, teachers, scientists, artists, musicians,
lecturers in the School of Civics and Philanthropy,
officers in The Juvenile Protective Association and in
The League for the Protection of Immigrants, a visiting nurse, a sanitary inspector, and others.

We have also worked out during our years of residence a plan of living which may be called cooperative, for the families and individuals who rent the Hull
House apartments have the use of the central kitchen
and dining room so far as they care for them; many
of them work for hours every week in the studios and
shops; the theater and drawing rooms are available for
such social organization as they care to form; the entire
group of thirteen buildings is heated and lighted from

a central plant. During the years, the common human experiences have gathered about the House; funeral services have been held there, marriages and christenings, and many memories hold us to each other as well as to our neighbors. Each resident, of course, carefully defrays his own expenses, and his relations to his fellow residents are not unlike those of a college professor to his colleagues. The depth and strength of his relation to the neighborhood must depend very largely upon himself and upon the genuine friendships he has been able to make. His relation to the city as a whole comes largely through his identification with those groups who are carrying forward the reforms which a Settlement neighborhood so sadly needs and with which residence has made him familiar.

Life in the Settlement discovers above all what has been called "the extraordinary pliability of human nature," and it seems impossible to set any bounds to the moral capabilities which might unfold under ideal civic and educational conditions. But in order to obtain these conditions, the Settlement recognizes the need of cooperation, both with the radical and the conservative, and from the very nature of the case the Settlement cannot limit its friends to any one political party or economic school.

The Settlement casts aside none of those things which cultivated men have come to consider reasonable and goodly, but it insists that those belong as well to that great body of people who, because of toilsome and underpaid labor, are unable to procure them for themselves. Added to this is a profound conviction that the common stock of intellectual enjoyment should not be difficult of access because of the economic position of him who would approach it, that those "best results of civilization" upon which depend the finer and freer aspects of living must be incorporated into our common life and have free mobility through all elements of society if we would have our democracy endure.

The educational activities of a Settlement, as well its philanthropic, civic, and social undertakings, are but differing manifestations of the attempt to socialize democracy, as is the very existence of the Settlement itself.

Index